Decolonising the Pale

Haidar Eid

Decolonising the

Palestinian Mind

First published in November 2023

LeftWord Books
2254/2A, Shadi Khampur
New Ranjit Nagar
New Delhi 110008
INDIA

LeftWord Books and Vaam Prakashan are imprints of
Naya Rasta Publishers Pvt. Ltd.

leftword.com

ISBN   978-93-92018-36-7 (paperback)
        978-93-92018-50-3 (e-book)

Printed and bound by Chaman Enterprises, New Delhi.

Contents

OCTOBER 31, 2023

Prologue One:

Even Ghosts Weep in Gaza

I am standing over the ruins of a house in Gaza City, peering at the horizon.

Most probably, the body of a martyr lies under the rubble. The body of someone who could not respond to an Israeli 'warning'.

Such 'warnings' are comprised of several artillery shells, missiles from a reconnaissance drone, followed by another missile from an F-16, a warplane made in the United States. A gift to the Palestinian people from a superpower.

Israel used to call some warnings a 'knock on the roof' — firing at a home to announce a larger attack was imminent. The 'knock on the roof' policy seems to have been stopped.[1]

In this house, a woman lived with her husband, three sons and three daughters. They had also provided refuge to relatives from northern Gaza who had been displaced.

Now, the house and the families who lived and took shelter in it are gone forever.

The adjacent house is 'luckier'. Its owner inspects it with a sense of astonishment.

1 'Senior Israeli source: Gaza will not be Hamastan; "roof knocking" policy no longer norm', *The Times of Israel*, October 9, 2023.

His neighbour screams when she sees all that she once owned turned into rubble because the US president believes that 'Israel has the right to defend itself'.

Defend itself against whom? Terrorists!

If Israel keeps killing at the rate it has been, the official death toll will reach 10,000 very soon. About 40 per cent of the dead are children.[2]

All terrorists.

'Human animals.'[3]

MAKE ME BE SUPERMAN

I imagine that my ghost is standing beside the ruins of another house in al-Rimal. Al-Rimal used to be a docile and peaceful neighbourhood in Gaza City.

My ghost pats one of my university students — a brilliant student — on the shoulder, offering her a tissue to wipe her tears. It embraces her father and carries her little sister, who weeps as she searches for their mother under the rubble.

Ghosts do not cry. My ghost is an exception.

This incident must be recorded as that of 'the first weeping ghost in history'.

My ghost sings to the pretty woman sitting on a rock in the middle of what was once a home. A home that contained dreams, hopes, and desires.

My ghost wipes her tears and weeps along with her.

My ghost reflects on the pain of birth.

My ghost goes to the Nuseirat refugee camp.

In Nuseirat, my ghost hears the cooing of a dove coming from

---

2 '40 per cent of Palestinians killed in Gaza are Children', *Defense for Children International – Palestine*, October 30, 2023.

3 'Israel cuts off food, water to millions of Palestinians it calls "human animals"', *The Electronic Intifada*, October 10, 2023.

the south, from Khan Younis. The dove bears the story of another home.

The home is a lover. A woman who has feelings for you and for whom you have feelings.

She is you, and you are her. There are no boundaries. No separation.

When the home is demolished, something within you dies.

'Where is my mom?' a little girl screams.

'Where is my dad?'

The girl is beside the rubble of yet another house — the rubble where the cooing dove had landed.

I try to pull myself together and fail.

My shadow refuses to return to my body. My ghost rebels against its master.

On *Laylat-al-Qadr* — the Night of Destiny — my prayer was: 'Oh God, make me be Superman during these massacres. I ask for nothing else, oh merciful God.'

Make me Superman, and I will not attack any Israeli, either soldier or civilian. I will not be aggressive towards either Benjamin Netanyahu or Itamar Ben-Gvir.

I will not even be aggressive towards Benny Gantz, who has boasted of sending Gaza back to the 'stone age' with all the slaughter he ordered in 2014.[4]

And I will not be any threat to Joe Biden or Rishi Sunak.

The only thing I will do will be to intercept the shells before they kill the children of Gaza.

My ghost decides to take leave. It is gone forever.

---

4   Ali Abunimah, 'Israeli election ad boasts Gaza bombed back to "stone ages"', *The Electronic Intifada*, January 21, 2019.

Prologue Two:

Audio Files from Gaza, Palestine

This book is being published while Gaza, where I live, is being annihilated. Amid the current genocidal attack carried out by apartheid Israel against the 2.3 million residents of Gaza, my wife, our two daughters (aged six and seven), and I were asked to leave our flat. We were trapped for about twenty-four hours in a very crowded, narrow room with at least twenty other people after being forced to flee our flat. We had no water, no food, no Wi-Fi, no data, no electricity. Israeli bombs are still raining down all around us.

Even after leaving my neighbourhood, which was flattened to the ground, we moved north, where I stayed for three days with my brother. And then we were asked, together with more than 1.1 million people, to head south, where I am staying right now in the southern city of Rafah. There are countless Palestinian doctors, nurses, teachers, bakers, artists, mothers, fathers, pensioners, ambulance-drivers, children, babies, such as my family, who have been forced to flee their homes and are now hiding in other rooms and flats in the southern part of the Gaza Strip, where many of us have been bombed too.

Israeli war crimes committed against our people in the Gaza

Strip are unprecedented, a combination of ethnic cleansing and genocide. Since Saturday, October 7, 2023, Israel has flattened neighbourhoods, including mine, and destroyed vital bridges, roads, residential towers, and villas on top of their owners. Water and electricity stations have also been shut down. Consequently, more than two-thirds of the population has been denied access to water and electricity. Children, the sick, and the elderly are the first to be affected. The latest from the Ministry of Health in Gaza is that more than 7,200 civilians have been killed, 65 per cent of whom are children and women. And there are thousands still under the rubble. Two-thirds of the population have been displaced. According to UNOCHA, 25 per cent of homes are either destroyed or damaged and 59 attacks on cultural centres and health centres, health care homes, including the Al-Ahli Al-Araby Baptist Hospital, in which 500 people were killed. All are going unnoticed by the so-called international community. More than 170 educational facilities, universities, schools, and educational centres were also bombed. Food, as scarce as it is, cannot be preserved. People are already experiencing severe dehydration due to lack of water. There is also an increasing threat of the spread of disease because of a lack of water.

The Palestinian people had already been under a hermetic medieval siege for the past seventeen years as collective punishment for exercising their democratic choice in elections in January 2006. Israel has turned the Gaza Strip into the largest concentration camp, with the largest population of prisoners in the world and called that 'withdrawal'. Unfortunately, the international conspiracy of silence towards the genocidal war taking place against the 2.3 million civilians in Gaza indicates complicity in these war crimes. In fact, Western governments — especially the United States of America (US) — are directly involved in these war crimes and crimes against humanity as evidenced by strong-worded statements made by the highest ranking politicians, the President of the US, the Secretary of State, the Secretary of Defence, Prime Minister of the

UK, President of France, Chancellor of Germany, Prime Minister of Italy — they all decided to visit apartheid Israel in a sign of total support for Israel's crimes against our people.

The failure of the United Nations and its numerous organisations to condemn such crimes committed by apartheid Israel proves their complicity. We have come to the conclusion that only civil society can mobilise to demand the application of international law and put an end to Israel's unprecedented impunity. Our inspiration is the anti-apartheid movement. The intervention of civil society *was* effective in the late 1980s against the apartheid regime of South Africa. Nelson Mandela, before his imminent death, and Archbishop Desmond Tutu, amongst other anti-apartheid activists, did not only describe Israel's oppressive and violent control of Palestinians as apartheid, but they also joined our call for the world civil society to intervene again.

We need to be more specific about our demands. Yes, I agree. We need to give clear-cut directions to what we exactly demand. And we want civil society organisations world-wide to intensify the anti-Israel sanctions campaign to compel Israel to end its genocidal attacks against us. It has become crystal clear that the international conspiracy of silence towards the incremental genocide and the ongoing genocide right now taking place against the 2.3 million civilians of Gaza indicates complicity in these war crimes. It is high time for the international community to demand that the rogue state of apartheid Israel, a state that has violated every single international law one can think of, end its medieval siege of Gaza and compensate for the destruction of life and infrastructure that it has visited upon the Palestinian people. But this should also come with a package of demands to be made by all Palestinian solidarity groups and supporters and all international civil society organisations that still believe in the rule of law and basic human rights.

We want an end to the occupation. An end to apartheid and other war crimes committed by apartheid Israel. An end to the siege that has been imposed on us since 2007. The protection of civilian lives and property as stipulated in international humanitarian law and international human rights law (such as the Fourth Geneva Convention). We need immediate reparations and compensation for all destruction carried out by apartheid Israel. We need to hold Israel's generals and leaders accountable for war crimes and crimes against humanity committed against us. And then, only then, can we start seriously thinking about a futuristic vision in historic Palestine where all people are treated equally in one state, a secular, democratic state for all regardless of religion and ethnicity.

Introduction

By writing this book, I am hoping to contribute to efforts made by other Palestinian activists, intellectuals, and writers and make it absolutely clear that we live in an 'as if' state that opens pathways to new worlds beyond the walls erected by apartheid Israel and its barbaric, inhumane policies. Paulo Freire would have called it 'untested feasibility', an elaborate philosophy of hope that called for marginalised groups to move beyond their 'limit situations' — i.e., the constraints placed on our humanity by Zionism — and, more importantly, how to transform those hostile conditions into a space for creative experimentation of freedom, equality, and justice. In sum, to emancipate. We also know from Aimé Césaire, Amilcar Cabral, Antonio Gramsci, Freire, Ghassan Kanafani, Edward Said, Frantz Fanon, Rosa Luxemburg, amongst other giant activists and intellectuals, that any action taken on the world necessarily transforms the world as we know it, and this transformation of the world affects the way we act on it afterwards. To enter this process is how individuals learn to become subjects who act upon a dynamic, open world rather than remaining passive objects that are merely acted upon in closed, unchanging systems, such as apartheid Israel, white South Africa, and Jim Crow in the US, want us to believe.

We have learned from many Palestinian heroes that ideas of liberation are not about static worldviews but also about world-changing, that apartheid and settler-colonialism can be defeated even with the smallest tools available.

Palestinian basic rights are non-negotiable.

Apartheid Israel has made it absolutely clear that since it

cannot get rid of us completely, we must become its inferior and colonised subjects forever. The majority of Israeli Jews support the genocidal policy of their government because, as Zionists living in a Jewish supremacist state, they are indoctrinated into believing that they are entitled to certain privileges that must be denied to the *goyim*, who happen to be the indigenous population of the land.

Ethnic cleansing was the solution to implement this racist ideology in 1948. And in 1967, a combination of colonisation and military occupation became the only option. The Israeli military's Proclamation Regarding Regulation of Administration of Rule and Justice no. 2 (1967) clarified that the Israeli General Military Commander would be in charge of Palestinian life:

All authority of government, legislation, appointment, and administration pertaining to the area or its residents will now be exclusively in my hands and will be exercised only by me or by any person appointed, therefore, by me or acting on my behalf.

No wonder then that almost all major, mainstream human rights organisations, including the UN Human Rights Council and the prestigious International Human Rights Clinic at Harvard Law School, have lately come to the conclusion that Israel is an apartheid state.[1]

Israeli apartheid, within this context, is a euphemistic word used to describe a multi-formed regime of oppression, one that denies the humanity of the colonised subject, namely native Palestinians. Despite this, in Gaza and Jenin, we refuse to march to

---

1 S. Michael Lynk, 'Israel's 55-year occupation of Palestinian Territory is apartheid – UN human rights expert', Press Releases, Special Procedures, UN Human Rights, March 25, 2022. S. Michael Lynk is the Special Rapporteur on the situation of human rights in the Palestinian Territory occupied since 1967.

Israel's death chambers sheepishly. We are not like the normalising Arab leaders who have accepted their inferior status because they refuse to recognise their oppression as injustice, instead accepting it as the order of existence.

In Jerusalem, Gaza, and other parts of historic Palestine, we have made it absolutely clear that we will fight the settler-colonial, apartheid regime that exists between the Jordan River and the Mediterranean Sea, a regime that has managed, successfully, to create a non-democratic state reality on the ground, thanks to the 1967 *Naksa* and the disastrous 1993 Oslo Accords. We believe that it is our right to demand that the international community support our struggle for justice and freedom; if the Europeans and North Americans believe that there is a just cause in Ukraine, why do they deny the justice of the Palestinian cause?

We, however, are aware that the tokenisation of our struggle and emancipation have, *alas*, become ordinary conduct on the part of organisations historically dedicated to the liberation of Palestine.

Once again, the Palestinian people are proving that they are more aware of the reality on the ground and more anxious for our rights than our leadership, right and left, and the so-called international community. The Ukrainian crisis has shown that it is our duty as Palestinians to create the alternative we need when, in fact, there is no existing political space that will accommodate our liberation. We are on the receiving end of a racist, Western onslaught that refuses to see any similarities between white, European Ukrainians and dark, Middle Eastern 'Ayrabs'. We, however, cannot compromise on our basic rights, including the right to self-determination and liberation away from the facade of talking independence and camouflaged racist solutions.

The question on every Palestinian mind (but not on the minds of the political elite) is: what are we going to do now that it has become absolutely clear that the so-called peace process allowed the production of new Israeli facts on the ground and new repressive practices that made a functioning Palestinian State essentially unviable?

As the Boycott, Divestment, and Sanctions (BDS) movement has maintained, those who make their support for BDS and its three demands, i.e. freedom, equality, and justice conditional on the movement's adoption of the so-called 'international consensus' (which is nothing more than an unjust solution dictated by Israel and the world's only current superpower, the US) are asking us to forfeit some of our basic rights as humans, which reveals a profoundly disingenuous position.[2] Our basic rights are not negotiable; solutions are.

One such solution that has been resurfacing is a secular-democratic state for all of its citizens.[3] This secular-democratic state would be established following the dismantling of the existing multi-tiered system of oppression between the Jordan River and the Mediterranean Sea. This solution guarantees political equality regardless of religious and ethnic backgrounds. This is precisely what the current upheaval in Palestine, led by revolutionary youngsters, is all about. The same slogans are being used in Gaza, Jenin, Jerusalem, Negev, Umm al-Fahm, and other Palestinian cities, slogans that represent a new consciousness that the older generation is unable to comprehend.

But this necessitates a serious Palestinian soul-searching starting from the infamous Oslo Accords before delving into strategies of resistance and futuristic visions of liberation.

---

2 Boycott, Divestment, Sanctions (BDS) is a Palestinian-led movement for freedom, justice and equality. BDS upholds the simple principle that Palestinians are entitled to the same rights as the rest of humanity.

3 The One Democratic State Campaign is a Palestinian-led initiative that calls for the end of the colonial Zionist regime and strives for the establishment of a single democratic state in historic Palestine, based on political, social, economic and cultural justice, in which Palestinians and Israeli Jews live in equality.

CHAPTER ONE

The Oslo Accords:
A Critique

In order to understand the Oslo Accords and the extreme damage they have wreaked upon the Palestinian cause, one needs a historical contextualisation of the so-called 'peace process'.

The Oslo Accords were claimed to be the first step towards self-determination and an independent state. But it is clear now, thirty years after the famous handshake on the White House lawn, that no state in the short run will be established — because of the mere fact that Oslo ignored the existence of the Palestinian people as a people. In other words, these accords have offered Zionism what it has always been striving for. Golda Meir's infamous statement that 'there are no Palestinians' is a case in point here.

And yet, claiming that 'Oslo' was a great opportunity and a 'break-through' and that the so-called 'peace process' was on track until the Palestinians blew it is a deliberate ideological distortion of reality, claiming to prepare Palestinians for yet more concessions.

Real comprehensive peace was not created in Oslo; rather, what was created was a US-Israeli plan to resolve the 'conflict' after the destruction of Iraq and the collapse of the Soviet Union and their attempt to construct a 'new Middle East' — to use

Condoleezza Rice's words — a Middle East characterised by US-Israeli hegemony and supported by Arab regimes.

The Oslo Accords were born dead because they did not guarantee the minimum national and political rights of the three components of the Palestinian people living in the Diaspora, Israel, and the West Bank and Gaza.

Comprehensive peace cannot be achieved as long as there are refugees, detainees, blockades, settlements, 'legal torture' of prisoners, dispossession, assassinations, and occupation. It is an illusion in the minds of those who signed the Oslo Accords.

FURTHER SUBJUGATION OF PALESTINIANS

These accords have led to the creation of a limited 'administrative autonomy' in the Gaza Strip and some parts of the West Bank. The local population was given 'the right' to form an authority that they could call 'national'. It has now become obvious that despite the famous handshakes on the White House lawn and the optimistic talk of the 'New Middle East', these accords have not guaranteed the establishment of a sovereign, independent Palestinian state, the return of the refugees, the demolishment of the growing Jewish colonies, compensation for Palestinians who have lost homes or property, the release of all political prisoners, or the opening of all checkpoints.

Nor did all the handshakes, kisses and friendly press conferences stop Israel from launching one of the bloodiest assaults in its history. In the Gaza War of 2009, Israeli forces killed more than 1,400 people, including 438 children, 120 women, 95 elderly people, 16 medics, five journalists, and five foreign women; destroying more than 40,000 institutions and houses, leaving many families homeless. And to add insult to injury, Israel's assault on Gaza in 2012 led to the killing of more than 150 civilians and injuring thousands more. That, of course, was not mentioned as an objective of the Oslo Accords, but nothing either was mentioned that would prevent such bloodletting from taking place.

This is the political reality that Palestinian officials who signed the agreement do not want to be reminded of. In fact, what has been created in parts of Gaza and the West Bank is a very strange entity — an apartheid-type Bantustan endorsed by the international community.

I would argue that Gaza (2009, 2012, 2014, 2021, 2023) is the mirror image of Oslo. One ought to remember within this context that 75-80 per cent of Gazans are refugees whose right to return is guaranteed under international law, a right that has been totally ignored by Oslo. In fact, what the accords have created in Gaza, and the West Bank for that matter, is two different worlds, both of which have been led by undemocratic institutions, many security apparatuses, military courts, corruption, mismanagement, inefficiency, and nepotism — to mention but a few (neo)colonial qualities.

By winning the 1948, 1956, and 1967 wars and getting international, Arab, and Palestinian recognition, Israel — as an apartheid settler-colonial state — has hoped to move onto a new stage, a stage that requires the forming of a 'new consciousness' among colonised Palestinians. Herein lies the danger of Oslo — the creation of a new paradigm through which the consciousness of the supposed enemy — the 'Other' — is washed out and replaced with a one-dimensional mentality through the construction of fiction — two states for two peoples — the goal of which is unattainable.

Put differently, to aim at creating the two-state Palestinian is to aim to create a false consciousness led by an assimilated intelligentsia, some of whom have a revolutionary past record. Singing the slogans of 'the two-state solution', 'two states for two peoples', 'return to the 1967 borders', or even 'a long-term truce' as proposed by Hamas —is intended to guarantee the subordination and conformity of the Palestinians. Gone is the right of return of six million refugees and their compensation, and the rights of the indigenous population of 1948 Palestine, now second-class citizens of Israel!

This goal, however, never sees the antithesis it creates as a result of displacement, exploitation, and oppression. It ignores the revolutionary consciousness that has been formulated throughout the different phases of the Palestinian struggle.

Nor does it take into account the legacy of civil and political resistance that has become a trademark of the Palestinian struggle. Hence, the necessity of the formulation of alternative Palestinian politics. To be conscious of the corruption of the Palestinian National Authority (PA) and of the huge class gap that the Oslo Accords have created has definitely been the beginning of de-Osloization represented in the issuance of the 2005 call for BDS — a call that has been endorsed by almost all Palestinian civil society, and the rise of calls for a secular, democratic state in historic Palestine, a single state for all of its citizens regardless of religious or ethnic background.

The Gaza Strip, however, is seen by the PA as one of three building blocks of an independent state, although it is geographically separated from the second, the West Bank. The third block, Jerusalem, is under total Israeli control. None of the Palestinians in the occupied territories believe that the 'semi-autonomous' zones in the Gaza Strip and the West Bank — that is, those that fall under Category A — can lay the foundation for an independent state. What Oslo has led to is, in fact, a new South African-style apartheid.

The tribal chiefs of the South African Bantustans used to believe that they were the heads of independent states. Luckily, despite its many compromises with the National Party, the African National Congress (ANC) had never accepted the idea of separation and Bantustans. At the end of the millennium, the official Palestinian leadership boasted of having laid the foundation for a Bantustan, claiming it to be an independent state in the making. For Zionism's continued presence in Palestine, the 'Other' must be assimilated and enslaved without becoming conscious of the enslavement. Hence the granting of 'semi-autonomous' rule over the most crowded Palestinian cities, and hence the logic driving the Oslo Accords.

Repeating the racist two-state mantra, carrying the Palestinian flag, singing the national anthem, and recognising Israel, regardless of the rights of two-thirds of the Palestinian people, are what Oslo is all about — and nothing else.

One of the most important outcomes of the Gaza massacres (2009, 2012, 2014, 2021, 2023) has been the unprecedented tremendous outpouring of popular support for the Palestinian cause; something the signatories of the Oslo Accords (1993) must not have been happy with. The return of the pre-Oslo slogans of liberation, as opposed to independence, have, undoubtedly, created a new dilemma, not only for Oslo political elites, but also for the NGO-ised Left.

The process of 'Osloization', i.e., a combination of corruption, NGO-isation, and a selling-out of revolutionary principles and sloganeering, fused with the fiction of the two-prison solution, was dealt a heavy blow in the 2006 elections. Judging from statements made not only by PA officials, but also by the Left, and even the Hamas government, the ultimate goal of the current river of blood has become the establishment of a Palestinian state in any dimension, i.e. the two-state solution. The contradiction between the tremendous international support, the revival of the BDS campaign, the outpouring of demonstrations against apartheid Israel and its war crimes against the Palestinians of Gaza, and the reiteration, by most political organisations, of the two-state mantra is a strong indication of the need for an alternative program that makes the de-Osloization of Palestine its first priority.

The lesson we learn from the repeated Gaza massacres over the last 12 years is to harness all efforts to fight the outcome of the Oslo Accords and to form a United Front on a platform of resistance

and reforms. This cannot be achieved without dismantling the PA and realising that ministries, premierships, and presidencies in Gaza and Ramallah are a façade not unlike the South African Independent Homelands with their tribal chiefs. The classical national program, created and adopted by the Palestinian bourgeoisie, has reached its end unsuccessfully. Most political forces, including the governing party in Gaza, fail to explain how six million Palestinian refugees will return to the Israeli State of the Jews, and how an independent Palestinian state will be created at the same time.

Hence, the necessity for an alternative paradigm that divorces itself from the fiction of the two-prison solution, a paradigm that takes the sacrifices of the people of Gaza as a turning point in the struggle for liberation, one that builds on the growing global anti-apartheid movement that has been given an impetus by Gaza 2009. De-Osloizing Palestine is, therefore, a precondition for the creation of peace with justice.

CHAPTER TWO

Israel as an Apartheid State

We had to wait for Israel's leading Human Rights organisation, B'Tselem's new position paper, *A regime of Jewish supremacy from the Jordan River to the Mediterranean Sea: This is Apartheid*, preceded by the Human Rights Watch Report, and followed by Amnesty International's devastating detailed research, to draw the attention of Western media outlets, the likes of *The Guardian*, *CNN*, and *The Washington Post*, to the fact that Israel, after all, is an apartheid state and that it discriminates against half of the population, which happens to be Palestinian, between the Jordan River and the Mediterranean Sea.[1] Not Edward Said, nor Archbishop Desmond Tutu and other South African anti-apartheid activists, or even the UN Special Rapporteurs on the situation of the human rights situation in the Palestinian territories occupied since 1967, Richard Falk and John Dugard — to mention but a few conscientious human rights fighters — were able to do that.[2]

1 *This is Apartheid*, Publications, B'Tselem, January 12, 2021; 'A Threshold Crossed: Israeli Authorities and the Crimes of Apartheid and Persecution', Human Rights Watch, April 27, 2021; 'Israel's apartheid against Palestinians: a cruel system of domination and a crime against humanity', Index Number: MDE 15/5141/2022, Amnesty International, February 1, 2022.
2 Richard Falk, *Palestine's Horizon : Towards a Just Peace*, London: Pluto, 2017; John Dugard, 'Why Aren't Europeans Calling Isarel an Apartheid State', *Al-Jazeera*, April 17, 2019.

It had to come from 'one of us,' white, middle class, and — most importantly — Israeli Jew.

Just a few years ago, the comparison with the apartheid regime of South Africa was considered taboo, thanks to the guilt complex originated from one of the worst pogroms in the history of humanity, namely, the slaughter of millions of innocent Jews at the hands of White, European bigots. The Whites of apartheid South Africa defined the institutions of the country as democratic — albeit white democracy, i.e., by and for whites only. However, the idea of defining the country as exclusively white and democratic at the same time was never accepted by the international community.

I happen to be a naturalised South African of Palestinian origin. I spent more than five years in Johannesburg, during which I earned a PhD from the University of Johannesburg. This is my background, experiencing two apartheids, one of which is lying at the bottom of the dustbin of history, while the other is thriving and basking in the glory of ethno-religious supremacy, aided and supported by ex-colonial and imperialist Western powers.

These same powers pay lip service to the suffering of the Palestinian people by repeating the mantra of the racist, two-state solution as if there are two symmetrical sides. Instead of calling a spade a spade and calling it settler-colonialism and apartheid, they insist on calling it the 'Israeli-Palestinian conflict'. But were there 'two-sides' to the South African 'conflict'? Were there two equal parties, namely White and Black, with equal claims to the land and equal historical responsibility for the-then status quo? No doubt, this sounds like a bizarre interpretation of South African history, which we Palestinians find equally astounding when applied to our history and our reality today.

The South African anti-apartheid goal, adopted by anti-apartheid activists all around the world, was unequivocal: the end of the racist system and ideology of apartheid. There could be no tolerance of apartheid practices; no creation of Bantustans: The system had to be dismantled in its entirety. Many South Africans, supported by a sustained global anti-apartheid campaign, sacrificed their lives to bring down the Bantustans, euphemistically called independent homelands by the apartheid regime. Like Black South African resistance, ours is morally superior to apartheid because it is inclusive where apartheid focuses on separation; it is embracing where apartheid focuses on division; it is life-affirming where apartheid is violent and murderous.

On the other hand, like apartheid South Africa, in the State of Israel, all human beings are NOT equal. There are fundamental artificially created and selectively rewarded levels of citizens in the state. Israel defines itself as a Jewish State.[3] It, therefore, creates a bizarre distinction between 'nationality' and 'citizenship'. Almost 22 per cent of the citizens of Israel are Palestinians who are excluded from such a definition. Thus, Israel is NOT the state of its citizens, but rather that of 'The Jewish People', most of whom have no birthright connection to it. All Jews, wherever they are born, enjoy full rights in Israel, rights that apartheid Israel denies to us, the indigenous people of this land. They also call us 'Israeli Arabs', 'Jerusalem residents', 'Arabs of the territories', not to mention the refugees living in the Diaspora, whose mere mention always spoils any party, and whose right to return and compensation is sanctioned by International Law (UNGA resolution 194).

Israeli nationality, therefore, is non-existent. Instead, there is 'Jewish Nationality'. This is not unlike emphasising 'White Nationality' as opposed to, say, South African nationality.

The International Convention on the Suppression and Punishment of the Crimes of Apartheid, Article 2, Part 3, clearly defines apartheid as:

> [A]ny legislative measures and other measures calculated to prevent a racial group or groups from participation in the political, social, economic and cultural life of the country

3 Raoul Wootliff, 'Israel passes Jewish state law, enshrining "national home of the Jewish people"', *The Times of Israel*, July 19, 2018.

and the deliberate creation of conditions preventing the full development of such a group or groups, in particular by denying to members of a racial group or groups basic human rights and freedoms, including the right to work ... the right to education, the right to leave and return to their country the right to a nationality, the right to freedom of movement and residence.[4]

This definition, in its entirety, clearly applies not only to the Palestinian people residing in the West Bank and Gaza Strip but also to those living in Israel itself. Hence, the importance of B'Tselem's conclusion: 'The entire area Israel controls between the Jordan River and the Mediterranean Sea is governed by a single regime working to advance and perpetuate the supremacy of one group over another'.

Furthermore, ICSPCA, Article 2, Part 4, makes it crystal clear that:

[t]he term 'the crime of apartheid', shall apply to 'any measures including legislative measure, designed to divide the population along racial lines by the creation of separate measures and ghettos for the members of a racial group or groups The expropriation of landed property belonging to a racial group or groups or to members thereof.

I, myself, am a resident of Gaza; like so many Palestinians, I have legal title to my parents' land in Israel, but have no 'legal' right to it because my parents' property, like that of millions of other Palestinians, was taken away from us and given over to Jewish ownership. The facts are that Jews owned only 7 per cent of

---

4 International Convention on the Suppression and Punishment of the Crime of Apartheid G.A. res. 3068 (XXVIII)), 28 U.N. GAOR Supp. (No. 30) at 75, U.N. Doc. A/9030 (1974), 1015 U.N.T.S. 243, entered into force July 18, 1976, UN. Org.

Palestine before 1948; today, 93 per cent is considered 'state land' and can only be owned by Jews or Israel.

It is time to call Israel to task, the same way the ugly apartheid regime was held accountable; it is time to heed the call made by the overwhelming majority of Palestinian Civil Society sectors and sanction apartheid Israel until it complies with international law by adhering to universal principles of equality and dignity.

TWO-STATE SOLUTION:
THE OPIUM OF THE PALESTINIAN PEOPLE

Saeb Erekat, chief Palestinian negotiator and Secretary General of the Executive Committee of the Palestine Liberation Organization (PLO), passed away at the age of 65. Some Palestinians have seen his death as a metaphor for the end of the Oslo era and its twisted logic.

Erekat and many Palestinian political functionaries of his generation have firmly stood by the so-called two-state solution, insisting that the Palestinians will be able to strike a fair deal with the Israelis and their US patrons to establish an independent Palestinian state on parts of historic Palestine.

The illusion that this is actually possible has been maintained through decades of continued colonisation and disastrous agreements. It is 'the opium of the Palestinian people'.

The accords with Israel signed by Egypt in 1978 at Camp David, by the Palestinians in 1993 in Oslo, and Jordan in 1994 in Wadi Araba were supposed to be necessary steps towards Palestinian self-determination and 'peace' in the Middle East.

But all these agreements ignored the existence of the Palestinian people as a people and their basic rights, including the right of return of Palestinian refugees and equality for Palestinian citizens of Israel.

Instead of insisting on those fundamental rights and following the example of South Africa's anti-apartheid movement, which mobilised international civil society around the idea of one person, one vote, and the establishment of a secular democratic, non-racial, non-sectarian state, the Palestinian political leadership reduced the Palestinian people to only those living in the West Bank, the Gaza Strip, and East Jerusalem.

This resulted in the formation of a Palestinian Bantustan of incongruous territories, where Palestinians live under the constant terror of a military occupation and where the PA does not actually exercise full authority.

The insistence on continuing down the Oslo path towards an illusory two-state solution has persisted even after Israel passed a Nation-State Law, in which it explicitly declared the right to self-determination in 'the Land of Israel' to be 'unique to the Jewish People' — i.e. according to the Israeli state, the Palestinians cannot enjoy that right. And it has persisted even as Arab states have pressed forward with normalisation with Israel without any concessions along the formula 'peace for land' and as the US has put forward yet another 'peace deal' in which it offers the Palestinians nothing more than humiliating subsistence.

Oslo and its derivative processes ignore the elephant in the room — the apartheid regime which Israel has effectively imposed on historic Palestine. They also do not pay attention to the consciousness of *sumud* (steadfastness) that has emerged out of the Palestinian struggle. Nor do they take into account the long Palestinian legacy of civil and political resistance.

Over the years, many Palestinians have come to see Oslo for what it is and have opted to draw alternative paths to secure Palestinian rights.

In 2001, just a year after the Second Intifada erupted, the NGO forum of the World Conference Against Racism (WCAR) was held in Durban, South Africa. It offered a very clear diagnosis of the nature of the Zionist project and paved the way for a much more practical but also progressive path to a new intersectional cooperation between the oppressed Palestinians and other marginalized groups.[5]

In 2005, the BDS Movement was created, and two years later, the BDS National Committee was formed to map its forward trajectory. BDS, along with the establishment of the One Democratic State Campaign and the Great March of Return — to give but a few examples — all represent the beginning of a process of de-Osloization of the Palestinian mind.[6] And in this process, Gaza has played a central role.

Most events that have taken place in the strip since the 2006 legislative elections represent an outright rejection of the Oslo Accords and their consequences. When we bear in mind that 75-80 per cent of Gaza residents are refugees, the anti-colonial and anti-Oslo context of the election results becomes that much clearer.

In the following years, the calls for an alternative paradigm that divorces itself from the fiction of the 'two-prison solution' intensified. It is a paradigm that takes the sacrifices of the people of Gaza as a turning point in the struggle for Palestinian liberation, one that builds on the growing global anti-apartheid movement that has been given an impetus by the 2009, 2012, 2014, 2021, and 2023 onslaughts on Gaza and by the Great March of Return.

The de-Osloization of Palestine, for most Palestinian activists, has become a precondition for the creation of peace with justice. That requires a redefinition of the Palestinian cause as an anti-colonial struggle against a system of settler-colonialism and apartheid, and reunification of the three components of the Palestinian people, namely, Gaza and the West Bank residents, refugees, and Palestinian citizens of Israel.

The first steps of this process were taken in Durban in 2001.

5   Maia Hallward, 'BDS and BLM: Positionality, Intersectionality and Nonviolent Activism', August 5, 2020.
6   For more on 'One Democratic State Campaign' please see footnote 9. Haider Eid, 'Back to the Future: The Great March of Return', *al-Shabaka*, July 24, 2018.

The Durban WCAR declaration, in a very peculiar way, demanded that Palestinians take up the most effective tool of international solidarity with their struggle to end apartheid in historic Palestine. The language used in the declaration was clear, diagnostic, strong, and — most importantly — uncompromising on basic human rights:

> We declare Israel as a racist, apartheid state in which Israel's brand of apartheid as a crime against humanity has been characterised by separation and segregation, dispossession, restricted land access, denationalisation, 'bantustanization' and inhumane acts.
>
> And this has, to all of us in Palestine, been the beginning of our South African moment, a step in our long walk to freedom, equality and justice.

ONE VS. TWO STATES

In August 2021, the influential US magazine *Foreign Affairs* carried out a survey on the two-state solution in Palestine among 'authorities with specialized expertise together with leading generalists in the field'.[7] It asked the question, 'is the two-state solution to the Israeli-Palestinian conflict no longer viable?' to which the 64 experts were supposed to indicate their agreement or disagreement and explain their stance with a brief comment. Of them, 32 disagreed that the two-state solution was dead, seven were neutral, and 25 agreed with the premise.

Some of those who disagreed are currently or were previously involved with Zionist-leaning think tanks, such as the Washington Institute for Near East Policy. Among them is former US ambassador to apartheid Israel, Martin Indyk, who served as a deputy research director for the American Israel Public Affairs

7 'Is the Two State Solution Still Viable?', *Foreign Affairs*, August 24, 2021.

Committee (AIPAC) before starting his diplomatic career.

The list also includes Dennis Ross and others who were heavily involved in the so-called 'peace process', an unending affair to secure the Israeli apartheid state and liquidate basic Palestinian rights altogether. Obviously, those who were part of the 'peace process' are still clinging to the illusion that it is possible to establish a Palestinian Bantustan.

Those who defended the two-state solution acknowledged that there are 'barriers' to its fulfilment; among those, the most frequently cited one was the 'lack of political will' on 'both sides'. There were even suggestions that the Palestinian leadership is solely to blame, as Hamas and the PA lack support from the Palestinian people to make the necessary sacrifices and accept Israel's apartheid and settler-colonial policies.

Interestingly, some of those who adopted the 'neutral' position preferred to take a postmodern, relativist stand on an issue that is one of freedom, equality, and justice — no more, no less. Others adopted a human rights approach to the Palestinian question, refusing to take a political stance.

What being 'neutral' on a clear-cut question of justice means can be anyone's guess. Just a few decades ago, who would have dared to be 'neutral' about the end of apartheid in South Africa?

In general, most of the supporters of the two-state solution in academia, foreign policy circles and beyond are Israeli, US, or European who do not see anything wrong with a settler-colonial project. The few Palestinians who are in favour of this racist approach to the Palestinian question fail to acknowledge facts on the ground: the system between the Jordan River and the Mediterranean Sea is a one-state reality, an apartheid state where one community has all the privileges of citizenship, while the other community is deprived of its fundamental human rights.

It is rather hard not to notice the racism and injustice involved in the apartheid reality in Palestine, where the Palestinians who suffer are not only the ones who live in the 1967 occupied territories, as the *Foreign Affairs* question implies.

I took part in the survey believing it was important to make my voice as a Palestinian heard. Here is what I had to say in the limited space provided:

> In addition to the fact that Israel has taken irreversible steps that have made this solution impossible — namely, the expansion of the Jewish-only settlements; the annexation of more West Bank lands in addition to Jerusalem; the construction of the apartheid wall that separates Palestinian from Palestinian; the blockade of the Gaza Strip; and the passing of the racist Nation-State Law by the Knesset — the two-state solution in principle does not offer the Palestinian people their basic rights under international law — equality and right of return. A Bantustan-like solution is a racist solution par excellence.

For such an influential US journal to raise such a question about the two-state reality in Palestine and make sure that there are some Palestinian voices among the respondents is very indicative of the power of the Palestinians to make their voices heard in the heart of empire. It is also revealing of the fact that the international discourse on Palestine is slowly but surely moving away from talk about the 'peace process' and the 'intransigence' of the Palestinian leadership.

This is clearly annoying the US and Israeli Zionists, with one survey respondent expressing his complete dismay at *Foreign Affairs* decision to even ask such a question. The defensiveness in the tone of many of the 'disagree' responses reveals that even staunch Israel supporters are realising that the two-state solution cannot resolve the Palestinian question, and it is already dead thanks to Israeli apartheid policies in Palestine.

The alternative is clear: one state for all inhabitants of historic Palestine, regardless of race, ethnicity, and religion; a state *a la* post-apartheid South Africa, one that is not based on the oppression of one community by another. A true solution to the Palestinian question cannot be reached by entertaining racist ideas about the separation of peoples. Only the restoration of Palestine's multicultural identity, one that is inclusive, secular, and democratic, can lead to lasting peace between the Jordan River and the Mediterranean Sea and beyond.

Herein comes Edward Said and his vision for a secular state.

CHAPTER THREE

Edward Said's Spectre and the End of the Two-State Solution

When the disastrous Oslo Accords were signed in 1993 on the White House lawn, Palestinian opponents were challenged by the signatories and their supporters: What is the alternative? As if this was the knockout question that would settle the debate regardless of the continuation of the settler-colonial nature of the relationship between the Israeli oppressors and the Palestinian oppressed.

The late Edward Said, a staunch opponent of the deal, took up the challenge in October 1993 and wrote a prophetic article in the *London Review of Books* titled 'The Morning After'.[1] Relying on what he called 'common sense', he simply predicted the situation which has developed since 1993; nothing more, nothing less. In a very eloquent style, he wrote:

In order to advance towards Palestinian self-determination — which has a meaning only if freedom, sovereignly and equality, rather than perpetual subservience to Israel, are its goal — we need an honest acknowledgement of where we are.

---

1 Edward Said, 'The Morning After', *London Review of Books*, vol. 15, no. 20, October 21, 1993.

What he found particularly 'mystifying' at the time, was 'how so many Palestinian leaders and their intellectuals can persist in speaking of the agreement as a "victory"'. The extent to which pro-Oslo intellectuals went in camouflaging the deal is epitomised by Nabil Shaath's description of the agreement as one of complete parity between Israelis and Palestinians.

In a series of articles in *Al-Ahram Weekly, Al-Hayat, Sharq Alawast,* and other papers and magazines, Said went on asking 'embarrassing' questions: Had Israel, under the Ashkenazi Zionist Labour government, decided to recognise the Palestinian people as a people when it signed the Oslo Accords? Were the Oslo Accords a radical change in Zionist ideology with regard to 'gentile Palestinian non-Jews'? Did the accords guarantee the restoration of a long-lasting comprehensive peace? And did the current leadership of the PLO represent the political and national aspirations of the Palestinian people? And in *The End of The Peace Process,* Said summed up these answers in response to the 'challenges' posed by Oslo intellectuals: 'No negotiations are better than endless concessions that simply prolong the Israeli occupation. Israel is certainly pleased that it can take the credit for having made peace, and, at the same time, continue the occupation with Palestinian consent'.[2]

We are reminded of these 'challenging questions' after President Abbas's 'historic' speech in which he declared an end to security cooperation with Israel and the US, due to Israel's planned annexation of parts of 30 per cent of the West Bank, eventually ending the Palestinian dream of having an 'independent' state on 22 per cent of historic Palestine. Independence was THE point of reference in any serious debate with pro-Oslo intellectuals, regardless of the price paid by the Palestinians. The problem, however, lay in the fact that what the Oslo Accords have led to, as

2 Edward Said, *The End of the Peace Process: Oslo and After,* New York: Vintage, 2001, p. 25.

has become a common fact now, is a situation that its signatories decided to ignore — the extreme difficulty — not to say impossibility — of establishing a sovereign independent Palestinian state on 22 per cent of historic Palestine.

The painful question now, in fact, is whether, since 1993, we have been forced to endure horrible massacres, a genocidal siege, the unstoppable annexation of our land, the building of an apartheid wall, detention of entire families and children, demolition of hundreds of homes, and many other abuses only because a comprador class saw 'independence' at the end of a closed tunnel?!

It is time now for us, opponents of the agreement, to throw the question back: what is the alternative? Or rather, was the deal itself ever a choice that would guarantee the minimum basic rights of the colonised Palestinian people, including freedom and self-determination?

Edward Said took up the challenge and wrote two pieces, 'The Only Alternative' and 'A Third Way' where he offered a solution based on 'equality or nothing', one that can be materialised in the establishment of a secular democratic state in Palestine in which ALL citizens are treated equally regardless of their religion, sex, and colour.[3,4] A comprehensive peace, for him, means that Israel, the colonising party, should acknowledge the right of Palestinians to exist as a people, their right to self-determination and to equality *ala* South Africa.

At the time, he asked whether 'the Palestinian leadership [was] listening? Can it suggest anything better than this, given its abysmal record in a "peace process" that has led to the present horrors?' Obviously, it wasn't!

---

3 Edward Said, 'The Only Alternative', *Al Ahram*, March 3, 2001.
4 Edward Said, 'Israel-Palestine: A Third Way', *Le Monde diplomatique*, September 1998.

EDWARD SAID AND THE RENDEZVOUS OF VICTORY

Since the beginning of the formation of his political consciousness in 1967, Edward Said has emerged as the world's most significant moral intellectual since Jean-Paul Sartre and Bertrand Russell. As a professor of literature and literary criticism and spiritual figurehead of the Palestinian cultural landscape, together with Ghassan Kanafani and Mahmoud Darwish, he was instrumental in moving Palestine towards becoming the most moral cause of our time. His dedication to Palestinian fundamental human rights elevated him to the status of icon and inspiration.

After the official leadership of the PLO signed the infamous Oslo Accords in 1993, Said began to argue that it was high time that the Palestinian people moved away from the illusion of the two-state solution and tried a democratic approach, one that could guarantee their basic rights, namely freedom, equality, and justice.

I was inspired by Edward Said because I belong to a generation that did not witness the *Nakba*, a generation that was thought to be resigned to more than fifty years of military occupation, more than seventy years of dispossession and apartheid. Herein comes Edward Said: a member of the *Nakba* generation with a different world-view, telling us something 'new' or rather reminding us, and the World, of the ABC of human rights, the Universal Declaration of Human Rights and the Geneva Convention, that Palestinians are worthy of freedom and self-determination like the rest of the peoples of the world. That can be achieved only in secular Democratic Palestine (even though I must admit, he was not clear enough about the differences between bi-nationalism and secular democracy as the most suitable solution). This is the way out of the quagmire created by Western Zionism in the heart of the Arab world.

We must admit that this was one of the major inspirational arguments behind our decision to rise up and resist. I am writing about Edward Said because after the passing of the racist Nation-

State Law by the Israeli Knesset, and Trump's declaration of the so-called 'deal of century', and the concrete steps taken to implement it, and the Israeli colonialist decision to steal a chunk of the occupied West Bank, and the deadly, medieval besieging of the Gaza Strip, we in Palestine have been reconsidering many of the taken-for-granted 'wisdoms'! But I also have been thinking about Aimé Césaire, Frantz Fanon, and Steve Biko — among other anti-colonial intellectual activists, and how they would have theorised our situation. Edward Said does that for us.

What would Said himself have said about what I call Palestinian neo-nationalism embodied in the Oslo Accords, signed by the right leadership of the PLO, and burgeoning in the last three decades with the encouragement and support of the EU, official Arab regimes, the US, and the World Bank which nominated one of its employees to the position of the prime minister of the PA? Palestinian neo-nationalism is about everything that beautifies occupation, endorses normalisation, and defends the racist two-state solution as THE solution to the Palestinian question regardless of the glaring fact that it denies the rights of two-thirds of the Palestinian people, namely refugees and Palestinian citizens of Israel.

Said, and all other anti-colonial heroes mentioned above, have very well-thought-out answers to those questions so-often raised about the alternative to this current deadly status-quo in Palestine as if there was no alternative to occupation, colonisation, and apartheid. My late mother, who was illiterate, summed it up very eloquently in 1993, the year the disastrous Oslo Accords were signed, and while many people took to the streets celebrating the deal that 'would bring about prosperity and turn Gaza into the Singapore of the Middle East', following instructions given by Osloized right-wing forces:do those agreements allow us (refugees) to return to Zarnouqa (the village from which she, together with tens of thousands, were ethnically cleansed by Zionist militias?).

Hence, our call for BDS and secular democracy in historic

Palestine was inspired first by the anti-apartheid movement and other struggles against settler colonialism and by the great ideas of those intellectuals, and I must add, freedom fighters. Freedom, Justice, and Equality or Nothing is our slogan. This is how we create space where Aimé Césaire put it, 'there's room for everyone at the rendezvous of victory'.

EDWARD SAID AND THE RE-DRAWING OF
THE (POST)-COLONIAL POLITICAL MAP OF PALESTINE

A re-reading of Edward Said's political writings — *The Question of Palestine* (1980), *The Politics of Dispossession* (1994), *Peace and Its Discontents* (1995), and *After the Last Sky* (1993) — offers an excellent starting point in formulating some of the questions (and answers) this article attempts to redress in its drawing of the (cognitive) political map of post-Oslo Palestine. Addressing the question of the (post) colonial, in this particular context, is a complex issue in that one seems to be dealing with a settler-colonist who denies his colonialism and argues to the contrary and with a victim whose victimization has been denied for decades. In order to understand the intertwined complex relationship between Israelis and Palestinians in a (post) colonial context, this chapter attempts to fill in the 'politico-ideological gaps' that have, deliberately, been concealed. In keeping with the spirit of Edward Said's work, this chapter maintains that the two-state solution under present conditions denies the possibility of *real* coexistence based on equality. This is because the Oslo Accords accept the Zionist consensus and, for the first time in the history of the conflict, seek to legitimise Israel as a Jewish state in historic Palestine. In these documents, therefore, Israel would appear to have been confirmed as the 'state of all the Jews' and never 'the state of all of its citizens'.

'Today, [Said's] words on Oslo are the soundings of a prophet.'
Sandy Tolan, 2013[5]

It is to the premise of Edward Said as a figure of dissent that I am inclined to subscribe in the course of this book. My task in this endeavour is to critically trace some of the ideas conducive to Edward Said being the oppositional intellectual, the *agent provocateur* in post-Oslo Palestine. It is what Said would call a 'contrapuntal reading' as a 'counter-narrative'.[6] It is a Saidian reading that attempts to understand the Oslo Accords, their disastrous consequences, and the power mechanisms that led to them. It is worth noting that Said's concern stems from the fact that as an 'Oriental' Palestinian who grew up in Egypt, Palestine, and Lebanon — all subject to the domination of the colonising West — he found it important to define the impact of the US, where he later received his education and which has had such a profound effect on his own life and that of all other Orientals.[7] As he says in the introduction to the re-edited version of *Orientalism*, he writes from the perspective of an Arab Palestinian with a strong concern and empathy for the region. This identification is obvious from such statements as this: '*Orientalism* is written out of an extremely concrete history of personal loss and national disintegration', recalling Golda Meier's 'notorious and deeply orientalist comment about there being no Palestinian people' had been made only a few years before he wrote the book in the second half of the 1970s.

In a series of articles and books distinguished for their inclusiveness, Said presents a profound and nuanced analysis of the Israeli-Palestinian 'conflict', following the eighteenth-century

5 Sandy Tolan, 'Edward Said and the Quest for a Just Peace', *Al Jazeera*, September 26, 2013.
6 Edward Said, *The World, The Text, and the Critic*, Cambridge: Harvard University Press, 1983, p. 47.
7 Edward Said, *Culture and Imperialism*, New York; Vintage, 1994.

Italian Philosopher Giambattista Vico's conviction that human culture, since it is man-made, can be positively shaped by human efforts. His consistent argument has been that what needs to be addressed with regard to the Zionist–Palestinian 'conflict' is an alternative representation that is necessarily 'secular' in its treatment of the Palestinian and Jewish questions — an alternative that never denies the rights of a people, one that guarantees total *equality* and that abolishes apartheid, bantustans, and separation in Palestine. In contrast with the mainstream media's *a*historical (mis)representation, his argument is a historical one. It is a reading which maintains that any attempt to understand the Oslo Accords, their consequences, and the power mechanisms that had led to them needs a re-reading of the close relationship between Zionism, US imperialism, and Arab reactionism.

Much has been said and written about the Oslo Accords. The signatories claim that these much-debated documents, in principle, opened up new possibilities for 'cooperation' between what has long seemed to be irreconcilable positions. Yasser Abed Rabbo and Yossi Beilin, the signatories of the Geneva Initiative, an extension of the Oslo Accords, believe that 'the *only viable* solution is a two-state solution' (my emphasis).[8] And, in what sounds like a warning, the latter adds that the window for a two-state solution will not be available indefinitely, and Israel will be forced to deal with the 'demographic threat' imposed on it by the Palestinians in historic Palestine.

The Accord and the Initiative have legitimized apartheid. Both documents include a language that is euphemistically reminiscent of the series of laws known collectively as the Group Areas Act (GAA), which forced the relocation of millions of non-white South Africans into racially specific ghettos. It was created to split racial groups up into different residential areas. As in apartheid South Africa, where the most developed areas were

8 Yossi Beilin and Yasser Abed Rabbo, *The Geneva Accord*, December 10, 2003.

reserved for the white people, and 84 per cent of the available land was granted to the same racial group, who made up only 15 per cent of the total population, in Palestine, even the 22 per cent of the historic land on which an 'independent state' is supposed to be declared is, according to the Oslo Accords, 'disputed'. In the South African case, the 16 per cent remaining land was then occupied by 80 per cent of the population. But contrary to the Palestinian case, the leadership of the indigenous population never gave that legitimacy.

Furthermore, is the establishment of an independent state as *the* solution to the Palestinian problem even possible? The leadership of the PA argues that *only negotiations* can solve it. For thirty years, negotiations have not moved the Israeli position at all; the Camp David negotiations reached the impasse predicted by both the Palestinian Left and the anti-Zionist Israeli Left. Ehud Barak's red lines are now very well known, and Benjamin Netanyahu's platform leads to nothing more than a canton for native Palestinians.[9] Add to this the fact that the establishment of a Palestinian state is not mentioned in any of the clauses of the Oslo Accords, thus leaving the matter to be determined by the balance of power in the region. This balance tilts in favour of Israel, which rejects the establishment of a sovereign Palestinian state despite its recognition of the PLO. No Israeli party, neither Left nor Right, is ready to accept a Palestinian state as the expression of the right of the Palestinian people to self-determination as defined by International Law. The Zionist Left is prepared to negotiate with the Palestinians in order to give them an advanced form of self-rule that will be called a state, and through which the Palestinians will be enabled to possess certain selected features of 'independence', such as a Palestinian flag, a national anthem, and a police force. Nothing more. This was Barak's 'generous' offer in Camp David in 2000, where American President Bill Clinton brokered Israeli-

---

9 Daniel Elazar and M. Ben Mollov, 'Elections 1999 – Character, Political Culture, and Centrism', *Jerusalem Center for Political Affairs*, 1999.

Palestinian negotiations to reach a final-status deal. The Right, on the other hand, is not prepared to give the Palestinians even these semblances of self-rule. Their vision of the future is rather that the Palestinians should be allowed to run their own affairs under strict and binding Israeli control.

But facts on the ground tell another story. In shocking statistics, Said shows how the successive governments of Israel had accelerated settlement expansion and land seizure in the occupied West Bank. He concludes, for example, that what the Israeli Prime Minister Ehud Barak's 'dovish' government was fighting for was the preservation of settlements, the maintenance of control over the Palestinian-occupied territories as a part of the 'Land of Israel', and the dominance of Palestinians through other Palestinians. Settlement activity in the West Bank continues, as do the confiscation of land and the opening of zigzag roads to service the settlements. Notably, the number of Jewish settlers has risen from 193,000, when the Oslo Accords were signed, to 600,000. (There are separate 'Jews only' roads for settlers and other roads for native Palestinians!). No Israeli government has ever been willing to commit itself to the complete evacuation of settlers from the West Bank. Yet this is a basic pre-condition for the creation of an 'independent Palestinian state', impossible in light of Israel's commitment to the settlers. In order to guarantee the security of the settlements and ensure their future development, Israel is bound to control the greater part of the West Bank and the Gaza Strip. Furthermore, in any future contingency, it is certain that Israel will invoke its security needs to justify tightening its control over the Jordan Valley, thus, again, rendering the project of an independent Palestinian state impossible.

This book maintains that, based on Edward Said's early reading of the accords, the two-state solution under present conditions denies the possibility of *real* coexistence based on equality. This is because the Oslo Accords accept the Zionist consensus and, for the first time in the history of the conflict, seek to legitimise

Israel as a Jewish state in historic Palestine. In these documents, therefore, Israel would appear to have been confirmed as the 'state of all the Jews' and never 'the state of all of its citizens'. The logic of separation implicit in these documents implies some fundamental contradictions and begs certain serious questions.

Jerusalem has suffered and is still suffering from the continuation of settlement activity, the building and expansion of Jewish neighbourhoods, the confiscation of Jerusalem IDs, i.e., ethnic cleansing, and the policy of 'facts on the ground' leaving no room for future Palestinian control over the city.

In addition, Palestinian refugees living outside the West Bank and the Gaza Strip are experiencing increasing difficulties, especially in places like Lebanon and Syria. They are waiting for the day to return to Palestine and to be compensated for their confiscated property. This is a right guaranteed by UN resolution 194. Meanwhile, the Palestinian community in Israel is prevented from coexisting on an equal footing with Israeli Jews. Israel's state policy against its Palestinian citizens amounts to apartheid as defined by the International Convention on the Suppression and Punishment of the Crime of Apartheid and ratified by United Nations General Assembly resolution 3068 (XXVIII) of 30 November 1973. Needless to say, the PA does not represent either of those two large segments of the Palestinian people.

Peace and Its Discontents (1995) and *The End of the 'Peace Process'* (2000) are about the unfolding situation in post-Oslo Palestine. The questions raised in these two collections of articles and essays are of paramount importance. Has Israel, under the Ashkenazi Zionist Labour government, decided to recognise the Palestinian people as a people when it signed the Oslo Accords? Are the Oslo Accords a radical change in Zionist ideology with regard to 'gentile Palestinian non-Jews'? Do the accords guarantee the restoration of a long-lasting comprehensive peace? And does the current leadership of the PLO represent the political and national aspirations of the Palestinian people? These are the kinds of questions Said tries to answer. He sums up these answers in what seems to be the gist of his latest books and articles about the Oslo Accords:

> no negotiations are better than endless concessions that simply prolong the Israeli occupation. Israel is certainly pleased that it can take the credit for having made peace, and at the same time continue the occupation with Palestinian consent.[10]

Oslo, therefore, has created what he called 'a kingdom of illusions.[11]

When *The End of the 'Peace Process'* was written, the Israeli prime minister at the time, Ehud Barak, supported the idea of the establishment of a demilitarized Palestinian state, or rather a Bantustan in most of the Gaza Strip and parts of the West Bank. Said holds that the programme of Barak's One Israel government did not challenge the *status quo* at the time, nor did it allow the Palestinian people to exercise the minimum of their national and political rights. Barak's clear platform during the elections, which he confirmed in his first victory speech, included his 'red line concessions':

> *NO* return to the borders of 4 June 1967;
> *NO* dismantling of the Jewish settlements in the Gaza Strip and the West Bank;
> *NO* return of Palestinian refugees;
> *NO* backing down on Jerusalem as 'the undivided, eternal capital city of Israel'; and
> *NO* unilateral declaration of an independent sovereign Palestinian state that can have a military on the western bank of the Jordan River. These reservations remain to be the platform of *all* Israeli governments, right and left, until today.

10 Edward Said, *End of the 'Peace Process'*, Granta Books, 2002, p. 25.
11 Edward Said, *Peace and Its Discontents*, London: Vintage Books, p. 148.

The so-called 'safe passage' that was established between Gaza and the West Bank was not free of 'interference from Israeli authorities', as mentioned in the Oslo Accords. Israel issued 'magnetic cards' — South African pass — required by Palestinians to travel on this 'passage'. Besides, Israel reserved the right to arrest any Palestinian 'suspect' on this route. Thus, the opening of the 'safe passage' did not change the enforced divisions between the Gaza Strip and the West Bank — divisions which have been enforced by Israel since 1991 and solidified since 2007, a fate predicted by Said in 1995 with the publication of his prophetic critique of the accords, *Peace and Its Discontents*.

Hence, the Palestinian state that Israel accepted is a Bantustan, a canton, a demilitarized state that lacks the necessary components of a sovereign, independent state, that is, a state that has a dependent economy, that lacks unified territory, and that it has no military power. But the *real* reality of what the Israelis were doing was putting the Palestinians on confined and controlled reservations, carefully and intensely restricting them from being able even to visit the great bulk of what just a few years ago was their country. According to Said, this is a state that will be accepted by the official leadership of the PLO, who, by signing the Oslo Accords, has completely surrendered to Israel.[12]

As argued earlier, the Oslo Accord was claimed to be the first step towards self-determination and an independent state. But it is clear now — almost thirty years after the famous ceremony at the White House — that no independent, sovereign state in the short run will be established because Oslo simply ignored the existence of the Palestinian people as a people. And if any Palestinian intellectual speaks out about this great injustice, they are automatically accused of 'terrorism' and 'incitement'. Hence, the banning of Said's *Peace and its Discontents* in the Palestinian-occupied territories.

12 Edward Said, *The Politics of Dispossession*, Chatto & Windus, 1994, p. 95.

Said argued consistently and convincingly that the Oslo Accords do not guarantee the establishment of a sovereign, independent state, nor the return of the refugees; nor the demolishment of all Jewish settlements, and compensation for those who lost — and are still losing — their homes, lands and properties; nor the release of all political prisoners; nor the opening of all checkpoints; nor free elections after the withdrawal of all Israeli troops from the territories which have been under occupation since 1967.

PALESTINE DE-OSLOIZED

Said compared the current situation in Palestine with apartheid South Africa — the tribal chiefs of the South African Bantustans used to believe that they were heads of independent states. Despite its many compromises with the National Party, the ANC never accepted the idea of separation and Bantustans. Said maintained that the Palestinian leadership, on the other hand, at the end of the millennium, boasts of having laid the foundation for a Bantustan, claiming it to be an independent state. This is undoubtedly the ultimate thing Zionism can offer to its oriental 'Other' after having denied their existence for a century, and after that same 'Other' has proved that they are human. For Zionism's continued presence in Palestine, the 'Other' must, therefore, be assimilated and enslaved without them being conscious of their enslavement. Hence the granting of 'semi-autonomous' rule over the most crowded Palestinian cities, and hence the logic behind Oslo.

Palestinian deterrence depends on the fact that they have what Said calls, 'the higher moral ground', and their victory at the end will be the inevitable result of their *sumud*, steadfastness, that has not wavered despite the feeling that they are left on their own.[13]

What is the Palestinian cause, if not the right of return of

13 Edward Said, 'The Only Alternative', *Al-Ahram Weekly*, March 1-7, 2001.

the refugees both inside and outside Palestine? Is there a slight possibility of having 'peace' in the Middle East without resolving this question? If, as some Israeli leaders claim, there is a way of finding a 'just solution' that does not include their return, does that guarantee a just, comprehensive peace?

The whites of apartheid South Africa defined the institutions of the country as democratic — albeit white democracy, i.e. by and for whites only. Native Africans never recognised the 'white nature' of that country. The idea of defining the country as exclusively white and democratic at the same time was never accepted by the international community. It was considered blatant racism.

That is precisely what the call for the recognition of Israel as a 'pure' Jewish state means. Forget about 6 million refugees scattered all over the world as a result of the process of 'ethnic cleansing' that accompanied the establishment of Israel in 1948.[14] According to this formula, informed by the Oslo Accords, the Palestinians are *only* those who live in the Gaza Strip and the West Bank. 'The Middle East conflict' will be resolved if the latter are given a flag and three to four truncated Bantustans with a chief that we can call a president.

THE BID FOR PALESTINIAN STATEHOOD

How would Edward Said have reacted to the Palestinian bid at the United Nations for statehood?

Certainly, he would have condemned the 'induced euphoria' that characterises discussions within the mainstream media around the declaration of an independent Palestinian state, which ignores the stark realities on the ground. Depicting such a declaration as a 'breakthrough', and a 'challenge' to the defunct 'peace process' and the right-wing government of Israel serves to obscure Israel's continued denial of Palestinian rights while

---

14 Ilan Pappé , *The Ethnic Cleansing of Palestine*, Oxford : Oneword, 2007.

reinforcing the international community's implicit endorsement of an apartheid state in the Middle East.

The drive for recognition has been led by Mahmoud Abbas, the Chairman of the Ramallah-based PA. It is based on the decision made during the 1970s by the PLO to adopt the more flexible program of a 'two-state solution'. This programme maintains that the Palestinian question, the essence of the Arab-Israeli conflict, can be resolved with the establishment of an 'independent state' in the West Bank and the Gaza Strip, with East Jerusalem as its capital. In this programme, Palestinian refugees would return to the state of 'Palestine' but not to their homes in Israel, which defines itself as 'the state of Jews'.[15] Yet 'independence' does not deal with this issue, neither does it heed calls made by the 1.4 million Palestinian citizens of Israel to transform the struggle into an anti-apartheid movement since they are treated as third-class citizens.

All this is supposed to be implemented after the withdrawal of Israeli forces from the West Bank and Gaza Strip. Or will it merely be a redeployment of forces as witnessed during the Oslo period? Yet proponents of this strategy claim that independence guarantees that Israel will deal with the Palestinians of Gaza and the West Bank as one people and that the Palestinian question can be resolved according to international law, thus satisfying the minimum political and national rights of the Palestinian people. Forget about the fact that Israel has as many as 573 permanent barriers and checkpoints around the occupied West Bank, as well as an additional 69 'flying' checkpoints; and you might also want to ignore the fact that the existing 'Jewish-only' colonies have annexed more than 54 per cent of the West Bank.

This same idea of 'independence' was once rejected by the

---

15 The distinction between 'nationality' and 'citizenship' in Israel confers on Jews who are not Israeli citizens greater rights and privileges in Israel than those conferred on Israeli 'citizens' who lack Jewish 'nationality'. This is a distinction unique in today's world, and not one normally associated with the word 'democracy'.

PLO because it did not address the 'minimum legitimate rights' of Palestinians and because it is the antithesis of the Palestinian liberation struggle. A state in name only is proposed in place of these rights. In other words, the Palestinians must accept full autonomy on a fraction of their land and never think of sovereignty or control of borders, water reserves, and, most importantly, the return of the refugees. That was the Oslo Agreement, and it is also the 'Declaration of Independence'.

Nor does this declaration promise to be in accordance with the 1947 UN partition plan, which granted the Palestinians only 47 per cent of historic Palestine even though they comprised over two-thirds of the population.[16] Once declared, the future 'independent' Palestinian state will occupy less than 20 per cent of historic Palestine. By creating a Bantustan and calling it a 'viable state', Israel will get rid of the burden of 3.5 million Palestinians. The PA will rule over the maximum number of Palestinians on the minimum number of fragments of land — fragments that Palestinians can call 'The State of Palestine'. Unlike South Africa's infamous Bantustans, this 'state' has already been recognized by tens of countries.

The much talked about and celebrated 'independence' will simply reinforce the same role the PA has played under Oslo. Namely providing policing and security measures designed to disarm the Palestinian resistance groups. These were the first demands made of the Palestinians at Oslo in 1993, Camp David in 2000, Annapolis in 2007 and Washington in 2011. Meanwhile, no commitments or obligations are imposed on Israel within this framework of negotiations and demands.

Just as the Oslo Accords signified the end of popular non-violent resistance of the First Intifada, this declaration of independence has a similar goal, namely ending the growing international support for the Palestinian cause since Israel's 2008-

16 See the map of Palestine according to the Partition Plan on
    https://www.un.org/unispal/document/auto-insert-208958/

2009 winter onslaught on Gaza and its attack on the Freedom Flotilla in May 2010. Yet, it falls short of providing Palestinians with minimal protection and security from any future Israeli attacks and atrocities. The invasion and siege of Gaza was a product of Oslo. Before the Oslo Accords were signed, Israel never used its full arsenal of F-16s, phosphorous bombs, and DIME weapons to attack refugee camps in Gaza and the West Bank. Over 1,200 Palestinians were killed from 1987-1993 during the First Intifada. Israel eclipsed that number during its three-week invasion of 22 days in 2009 when it managed to kill more than 1,443 people in Gaza alone. All in all, it has reinvaded Gaza four more times over the last decade, killing more than 4,000 civilians. This does not include the victims of Israel's siege in place since 2007, which has been marked by closures and repeated Israeli attacks before the invasion of Gaza and since.

As Saree Makdisi puts it:

In the wake of Mahmoud Abbas's UN General Assembly speech . . . it was clear to many Palestinians that the statehood bid was not really intended to address or secure the rights of all Palestinians, but rather to . . . tactically reframe rather than strategically transform the pointless negotiations game that he and his associates have been playing for two decades now.[17]

Ultimately, what this 'declaration of independence' offers the Palestinian people is a mirage, an 'independent homeland' that is a Bantustan-in-disguise. Although it is recognised by many friendly countries, it stops short of providing Palestinians with freedom and liberation. Critical debate — as opposed to one that is biased and demagogic — requires scrutiny of the distortions of history through ideological misrepresentations. What needs to

---

17 Saree Makdisi, 'The Power of Narrative: Reimagining the Palestinian Struggle', *After Zionism: One State for Israel and Palestine*, eds. A. Lowenstein and A. Moore, London : Saqi Books, 2012, pp. 91-92.

be addressed is a historical human vision of the Palestinian and Jewish questions, a vision that guarantees complete *equality*, and abolishes apartheid —instead of recognising a new Bantustan after the fall of apartheid in South Africa.

SAID'S VISION: ONE STATE FOR ALL

What I have tried to do is to show that the Palestinian experience is an important and concrete part of history, a part that has largely been ignored both by the Zionists who wished it had never been there, and by the Europeans and Americans who have not really known what to do with it. I have tried to show that the Muslim and Christian Palestinians who lived in Palestine for hundreds of years until they were driven out in 1948, were unhappy victims of the same movement whose whole aim had been to end the victimization of Jews by Christian Europe. Yet it is precisely because Zionism was so admirably successful in bringing Jews to Palestine and constructing a nation for them that the world has not been concerned with what the enterprise meant in loss, dispersion, and catastrophe for the Palestinian natives.[18]

In order to understand all the events that have been taking place in post-Oslo Palestine, including the wars on Gaza in 2009, 2012, 2014, 2021, and 2023, one ought to trace their origin back to 1948. Of importance within this context is the reminder that two-thirds of the Palestinians of Gaza are refugees who were kicked out of their cities, towns, and villages in 1948. In *After the Last Sky* (1993), Said argues that every Palestinian knows perfectly well that what has happened to us over the last six decades is 'a direct consequence of Israel's destruction of our society in 1948'.[19]

The problem, he argues, is that a clear, direct line from our

18 Edward Said, *The Question of Palestine*, London: Routledge, 1980, p. xxxiv.
19 Edward Said, *After the Last Sky*, London: Vintage, 1980, p. 5.

misfortunes in 1948 to our misfortunes in the present cannot be drawn, thanks to 'the complexity of our experience'. Therefore, there is an urgent need to counter the Nakba to achieve peace with justice.

Nonetheless, Said is not against a political solution in principle. On the contrary, he holds that a minimum fair solution at this stage must be based on resolutions of international legitimacy which accord the Palestinian people some of their rights — i.e., self-determination, establishment of an independent state, return of dispossessed refugees and Jerusalem, and the removal of the Jewish settlements. However, ironically, what the Oslo Accords have led to is a situation that its signatories did not envisage, that is, the extreme difficulty — not to say impossibility — of establishing a sovereign independent Palestinian state on 22 per cent of historic Palestine. Hence, his defence of the establishment of a secular democratic state in Palestine-Israel in which ALL citizens are treated equally regardless of their religion, gender, and colour. A comprehensive peace, for him, means that Israel — which dispossessed 800,000 Palestinians in 1948; occupied the West Bank, Gaza, Golan, and Sinai in 1967; annexed Jerusalem and Golan; invaded Lebanon in 1982; expropriated Palestinian land, built settlements; killed more than 2000 Palestinians during the Intifada (1987-1993); uprooted trees, assassinated Palestinian leaders; banned books; demolished houses; closed universities — should acknowledge the right of Palestinians to exist as a people, their right to self-determination. What Said found 'astonishing' is how far, after more than 60 years, supporters of Israel will go to suppress the fact that these years have gone by without Israel's restitution, recognition, or even acknowledgement of Palestinian human rights and without connecting that suspension of rights to Israeli official policies.

As mentioned earlier, there is no Israeli nationality, while Israel continues to define its national character as Jewish and not Israeli, which effectively excludes all Palestinians and 'non-Jews' living in Israel. This, as noted by the UN Committee on Social, Economic, and Cultural Rights, 'encourages discrimination and accords second class status to [Israel's] non-Jewish citizens'.

Defending a two-state solution is, therefore, an insult to the memory of those who fought for equality and justice not only in Palestine but also in the US South and South Africa. Thus, Said concludes that a sovereign, independent Palestinian state is, for the reasons mentioned above, unattainable. The question, therefore, is whether there is an alternative solution? One alternative increasingly to be found in Said's writings and pronouncements is the idea of a secular-democratic state in Mandatory Palestine in which all citizens are treated equally regardless of their religion, race, or gender.

A secular, democratic state is one inhabited by its citizens and governed on the basis of equality and parity both between the individuals as citizens and between groups which have cultural identities. Inherent in such an arrangement is the condition that the groups living there are enabled to coexist and develop on an equal footing.

This system is proposed here as a long-term solution that will need much nurturing, following the political demise of the project of an 'independent Palestinian state' as a result of the Oslo Accords, the siege of the Gaza Strip, and the occupation of the West Bank. The International Community considered the establishment of Bantustans in South Africa to constitute a racist solution that could not and should not be entertained. In order to bring that inhumane solution to an end, the apartheid regime was boycotted academically, culturally, diplomatically, and economically until it succumbed and crumbled into pieces. Nothing remains of the old ethnically cleansed South Africa or the impoverished Bantustans it had created: not the red carpets, nor the national anthems, or the security apparatuses. This is what racist solutions come to — a corner in the dustbin of history — a museum for the gaze of new generations.

A serious, comprehensive solution to the Palestinian question will not, therefore, neglect the 1948 Palestinians and those who were expelled and dispossessed of their lands in 1948, namely, refugees living in miserable camps. The mechanism by which such serious issues can be resolved is not a Bantustanisation *a la* apartheid South Africa as suggested by the signatories of the Oslo Accords. Rather, a secular democratic state where *all* citizens are treated equally is the right solution to end the conflict. This is what Edward Said's political vision is about; a vision that some Palestinian and Israeli activists have taken up.[20]

Edward Said, the political activist, is what the official Palestinian leadership is *not*. Said was charisma combined with a political vision and a clear-cut ideological programme. Whereas the Palestinian leadership is prepared to recognise a 'Jewish state' alongside a Palestinian State regardless of what this means, namely the discriminatory practices applied by Israel against its non-Jewish, i.e. mainly Palestinian citizens and residents since 1948, Said's alternative makes the necessary link between all Palestinian struggles against the occupation of Gaza and the West Bank and against Israel's ethnically-based displacement, dispossession, discrimination, and rights violations of more than one million Palestinian citizens, including some 250,000 internally displaced, as well as the 1948 externally displaced refugees, who are entitled to return, restitution, and Israeli citizenship under international law. The Palestinians, for him, are one people with one cause; to achieve a just peace, the rights of *all* Palestinians must be addressed. So, as Saree Makdisi maintains in his argument about the necessity for a one-state solution, if Palestinians declare that all they want is a state in the West Bank and Gaza, then that relieves Israel of the

---

20 Such as Ali Abunimah, *One country: A bold proposal to end the Israeli-Palestinian impasse*, New York: Metropolitan Books, 2006; Abdel Bari Atwan, *A Country of Words*, London: Saqi Books, 2008; Omar Barghouti, 'A secular democratic state in historic Palestine: Self determination through ethnic decolonisation', *After Zionism*.

challenges of democratic and equal rights for all citizens, including returned refugees.

Hence the calls, inspired by the legacy of Edward Said, amongst Palestinian activists in post-Oslo Palestine for an alternative paradigm that divorces itself from the fiction of the two-state or two-prison solution, a paradigm that takes the sacrifices of the people of Gaza as a turning point in the liberation struggle, one that builds on the growing global anti-apartheid movement. De-Osloizing Palestine, for most Palestinian activists, has become a precondition for the creation of peace with justice.

CONCLUSION

For Said, coexistence in Palestine-Israel is unachievable at the present moment because Israel is *not* the state of all its citizens, but rather the state of Jews entitled to the 'entire land of Israel', and because there has been no serious attempt on the Israeli side to acknowledge the right of the 'Other' to exist as an equal partner. How are Palestinians, whose entire territory was occupied, and society destroyed, who now live under worse conditions, and whose leadership has acknowledged Israel's right to exist, supposed to deal with the US-Israeli understanding of 'comprehensive peace?'. How are they supposed to coexist with a state that still has not declared its boundaries?

To put it differently, has there been any change in the colonialist and exclusivist behaviour of Israel as a settler colony that indicates that it is somehow prepared to (co)exist in the midst of the Arab world? These are the kinds of questions that Said thinks need to be addressed instead of 'blaming the victims' for the mere fact of being victims. At the core of comprehensive peace is justice, non-discrimination, and equality — qualities that Israel denies all Palestinians.

In post-Oslo Palestine, Said remains the controversial 'amateur', public intellectual who speaks truth to power. As he puts it in his discussion of the role of resistance: [it] only takes a few bold spirits to speak out and start challenging a *status quo* that gets worse and more dissembling each day'.[21] Interestingly, his work has consistently striven 'to cross rather than to maintain barriers'.[22] His writings on Palestine, in particular, and on the post-colonial world in general, are a Gramscian manifestation of the pessimism of the intellect and the optimism of the will.

21 Said, *The End of the 'Peace Process'*, p. 26.
22 Said, *The Politics of Dispossession*, p. 336.

CHAPTER FOUR

The Crisis of Palestinian Representation

The ongoing debate amongst Palestinians on Palestinian representation thirty years after the signing of the Oslo Accords requires a historic-political contextualisation. It is almost impossible to delve into the representation crisis without understanding the damage caused to the Palestinian cause by the infamous Oslo Accords. The question of Palestinian refugees was not even included in these agreements, and decisions on such critical issues were left to the time when both sides would negotiate the so-called Final Status Agreement. This chapter will examine how the Palestinian centres of power changed on the twenty-first anniversary of the Oslo Agreement. It will also explore the relationship between Palestinians inside and outside Palestine in light of the complete failure of the political process.

INDEPENDENCE VS BANTUSTANIZATION

The 'euphoria' that characterised discussions within the mainstream media around the declaration of an independent Palestinian state, ignores the stark realities on the ground and the warnings of critical commentators. Depicting such a declaration as a 'breakthrough', and a 'challenge'to the defunct 'peace process' and the right-wing government of Israel serves to obscure Israel's continued denial of Palestinian rights while reinforcing the international community's implicit endorsement of an apartheid state in the Middle East.

Ironically, this same idea of 'independence'was once rejected by the PLO because it did not address the'minimum legitimate rights'of Palestinians and because it is the antithesis of the Palestinian struggle for liberation. What is proposed in place of these rights is a state in name only. In other words, the Palestinians must accept full autonomy on a fraction of their land and never think of sovereignty or control of borders, water reserves, and most importantly, the return of the refugees. That was the Oslo Agreement, and it is also the much-celebrated 'Declaration of Independence'.

One can only assume that the much-talked-about 'independence' will simply reinforce the same role that the PA played under Oslo — namely, providing policing and security measures designed to disarm the Palestinian resistance groups. These were the first demands made of the Palestinians at Oslo in 1993, Camp David in 2000, and Annapolis in 2007. Meanwhile, no commitments or obligations are imposed on Israel within this framework of negotiations and demands. In fact, Israel's position is best spelt out by its right-wing Prime Minister, Benjamin Netanyahu:

The [Israeli] demand[s] [are] that Palestinians recognize Israel as the national homeland of the Jewish people; a commitment to end the conflict; a solution to the Palestinian refugee issue that did not require absorption within Israel's borders; the establishment of a Palestinian state only in accordance with a peace deal that did not infringe on Israel's security; that said Palestinian state be demilitarized; the preservation of large settlement blocs within the West Bank; and the insistence that Jerusalem remain the undivided capital of Israel.[1]

Just as the Oslo Accords signified the end of popular non-violent resistance to the First Intifada, the declaration of independence has a similar goal, namely ending the growing international support for the Palestinian cause since Israel's 2008-2009 winter onslaught on Gaza and its attack on the Freedom Flotilla in 2010. Yet, it falls short of providing Palestinians with minimal protection and security from any future Israeli attacks and atrocities. The 2009, 2012, 2014, 2021, and 2023 invasions and siege of Gaza were a product of Oslo.

Ultimately, what the 'declaration of independence' offers the Palestinian people is a mirage, an 'independent homeland' that is a Bantustan-in-disguise. Although it is recognised by so many friendly countries, it stops short of providing Palestinians freedom and liberation, which entail the return of Palestinian refugees who are supposedly represented by the PLO and its institutions.

REPRESENTATION

Following assurances and promises by US President George W. Bush and British Prime Minister Tony Blair to spread democracy in the Middle East, only to go on to cause the destruction of Iraq and Afghanistan, a third of the Palestinian population (those in the 1967 territories) voted against the existing PA government, led by Fatah. Instead, they voted in favour of what seemed then to be the only political force capable of challenging the remnants of the Oslo Accords. They did not vote based on their own political perspectives but rather to punish an authority characterised by corruption, suppression of freedom, de-prioritisation of the national struggle, security coordination under the oversight

---

1 'Netanyahu: Israel Willing to "Cede Parts of Our Homeland" for True Peace', *Haaretz*, May 16, 2011.

of a US general, the steady growth of layers of unproductive bureaucracy and a comprador class, suppression of the national forces of opposition parties, and most importantly, *minimisation of the Palestinian people to the population of the West Bank and Gaza.*

Add to this the transformation of Palestinian national aspirations through the marginalisation of the Palestinian Liberation Organization and the establishment of an'independent' Palestinian mini-state on a fraction of the land of historic Palestine — recognition of Israel but without asking Israel to reciprocate and recognise the rights of the Palestinian people, and thereby bestowing legitimacy on the Zionist project. This process had been unprecedented in the history of national liberation movements. In Palestine's unique case, the oppressed colonised accepted the process of Bantustanization, ceding to the oppressive coloniser 78 per cent of the land.

In order to complete this fallacy and reinforce the new reality that emerged after 1993, they had to create new institutions reflecting the supposed equality between the two parties, and sell the illusion of 'independence' to the Palestinian people. Among these institutions was the Palestinian Legislative Council (PLC), which represents *only* West Bank and Gaza Strip residents.

When the first elections were held in 1996, most left-wing and Islamic forces boycotted them, for reasons largely consistent with what is proposed by this argument and which remain valid; namely, the impossibility of voting freely, choosing your candidate under the threatening gun of the occupier. History has never witnessed such a process, unless we consider Afghanistan and Iraq to be free countries. But the election result was known in advance: It would be difficult, if not impossible, for a political force consistently opposing the Oslo agreements to win a majority of seats in the new Legislative Council. As expected, 'victory' went to the right-wing political force that had signed the Accords, with some token opposition included to complete the picture. This illustrates the reason for the resignation of much-respected Gaza-based leader Dr Haidar Abdel-Shafi from the Legislative Council, and also explains the massive and effective opposition from the late Edward Said to the accords as a whole.

Despite the non-participation of many political forces from the religious right and the left, an enormous change in the political culture of Palestine took place, reflected in the emergence of new terms — 'a culture of dialogue', 'recognition of the other', 'empowerment', and 'NGOization' — accompanied by favours to those in power and the elevation of the security services, now considered as an extension of the revolution and resistance. All this contributed to the spread of the Oslo virus, which infected the political powers that had previously refused them. This paved the way for broader participation in the 2006 elections, based on the possibility of change from within, adaption to the new reality created by the agreements, and hopes for forming a strong opposition from within, etc. Reasons cited to explain the lack of participation in the 1996 elections were completely ignored.

The Palestinian residents of the West Bank and Gaza went to the polls again, but this time in order to avoid repeating the outcome of the previous election, and to repudiate the PA and its governing party. Their defeat brought great joy that the *status quo* had successfully been ended. And then the problem became the religious right, who won the elections, but forgot that many of those who voted for them were not necessarily supporters of their political — or particularly ideological — programme; they ignored the fact that they had won the votes of a percentage of the residents of the West Bank and Gaza only.

The formerly Left, now turned neoliberal NGO, had decided to join the 2006 elections due to the fact that it had been historically marginalised by the secular right-wing leadership of the PLO and then got infected by the 'new' political culture. Some of its revolutionary leaders were eliminated, arrested, and some even handed over to the Occupation. This would cost them dearly, as evidenced by the very few votes they got in 2006.

The results of the PLC elections were 'a surprise' if not a blow to the domination of imperialism, Zionism, and the Arab reactionary regimes in spite of all the money poured into advertising campaigns attempting to consolidate the same culture that had prevailed for over a decade — the culture of Camp David and Taba, and Gaza — Jericho first, and Oslo, and Wadi Araba — a culture based on ethno-religious partition, two states for two peoples, a culture of, what I call in a different context, 'Osloization.' During its apartheid era, South Africa was similarly partitioned into five 'countries', four of which were Bantustans, for five 'peoples'. White South Africa controlled 88 per cent of the land and resources, leaving little for the natives. As argued earlier, the Palestinian signatories of the Oslo Accords were aspiring to establish an elusive 'independent state' on 22 per cent of the land.

But, the outcome of the 2006 elections carried a clear message against this political logic, and it came as a surprise even to those who won a majority of seats. The Oslo Virus, however, continued to infect even the victorious right-wing, religious political party that had won through its opposition to such agreements — but by disregarding the principle that participation in the elections is in itself a tacit approval of the foundations on which they were held.[2] Alas, it was forgotten that the PLC is one of the institutions, amongst others, including the PA itself, with its 'ministries' and security apparatuses that had emerged from the Oslo agreements.

As the election result ran contrary to the scenario envisioned by the US and Israel, it was necessary to punish the Palestinian voter, who had dared to take a lie — the spread of democracy in the Middle East — seriously. The result was inevitable: long-lasting and horrific, a crippling blockade was imposed on the Gaza Strip

2   Haider Eid, 'The Oslo Virus and the Struggle for Bantustans', *Palestine Chronicle*, November 9, 2010.

by land, sea, and air, with the participation of the deposed dictator Hosni Mubarak. This blockade, in its diverse forms, has caused the deaths of thousands of patients denied lifesaving treatments, continuous power interruption, an unprecedented medical crisis, the prevention of travel through the seven crossings that divide the Gaza Strip from the outside world, scarcities of fuel supplies, and the prevention of the imports of textbooks and other materials — milk foremost among them. There is no room here to write at length about this medieval siege, but the then United Nations Special Rapporteur for Human Rights in the Occupied Territories, Richard Falk, summarized its intent by calling it —'a prelude to genocide' and 'a Holocaust in the making'.[3]

This is exactly what happened two years after the first transparent and fair elections in Palestinian history. The siege failed to subjugate the Palestinians of Gaza; on the contrary, it has entrenched a culture of resistance in multiple forms. Israeli occupation forces, therefore, soon waged an unprecedented onslaught on the Gaza Strip, causing the deaths of thousands of its inhabitants, hundreds of them children killed in broad daylight, with no response of outrage from the so-called international community and the Arab reactionary regimes.

In spite of this high price and the enormous sacrifices they meant, the Palestinian people did not kneel. But the question here relates to the most prominent link between the 2006 election and the price paid by ordinary people for its outcome. The equation has become clear: if you go to the ballot box and elect against the continuation of 'dialogue' with Israel, through a US-brokered process, you will face a crippling blockade, accompanied by brutal genocidal wars, with the finger of blame pointed at you.

Just as the 1996 elections did not lead to an independent Palestinian state on the 1967 borders with Jerusalem as its capital, the 2006 elections similarly did not lead to either independence

3 Richard Falk, 'Slouching Towards a Palestinian Holocaust', *Zaman*, July 10 and 11, 2007.

or liberation, despite its dramatically different outcome. On the contrary, each election birthed an authority that did not enjoy any form of sovereignty unless we consider flags, red carpets, the national anthem, and the title of Prime Minister — the most critical manifestations of sovereignty.

The 1996 election cemented and legitimised the division of the West Bank into Bantustans, continuing the established pattern of the infamous apartheid system, naming its regions 'A, B, and C', and creating a national authority that represents the Palestinians of the West Bank and Gaza Strip, and whose only task was to implement repressive security measures against its opponents and elevate the idea of 'independence' at the expense of the right to self-determination, thereby dealing with only one form of oppression, namely the Israeli military occupation of the West Bank and Gaza Strip. Even this worsened since these regions were now acknowledged as 'disputed'.

The 2006 election, however, has spawned another, albeit unwanted, authority, entrenched in the Gaza Strip and playing the role of prison sergeant or chief of prisoners, regulating the lives of 2 million prisoners. The new winners made many attempts of the elections to appease the US through messages reassuring it, and emphasising, more than once, from the lips of the most prominent leaders, their willingness to accept an independent Palestinian state on the 1967 border, without recognition of Israel. Hamas even changed its charter to accommodate conditions imposed on it by the Quartet. This Osloized pragmatism has been accompanied by the application of strict religious laws, without formally legalising them, reflecting the new rulers' ideological background, but under the claim that they sought 'the protection of customs and traditions'. Day by day, we have seen this authority shift from a stage of resistance to the siege, to coexisting with it and finally reaching a stage of taking advantage of it. It has created a new, unproductive, rentier class whose capital is based on trade in the tunnels (before their destruction by the Egyptian authorities), land trading, a monopoly on the marketing of building materials, etc. This went hand in hand with a monopoly on the definition of resistance, excluding the possibility of reconciliation with those who do not follow its ideology.

As part of the falsely constructed binary between these two authorities, came the call to prepare for new PLC elections as part of a new reconciliation agreement between them. The choice again was between the religious right and the secular right, with a third, necessary alternative absent. What was the desired outcome of these elections? And would they be radically distinct from those of their predecessors? Were they meant to address the crucial mistakes that plagued the previous two elections or resulted from them? This time, would the right to self-determination, as defined by every Palestinian, appear on the ballot? In other words, would the electoral process include all the sectors of the Palestinian people and their aspirations, or would it, like its predecessors, be exclusionary and limited? Would it help to deconstruct the fetish of 'independence' away from foreign intervention?

In other words, would they be free elections even though they would be held, once again, under the barrel of the gun of the occupier? Would they reflect the genuine desires of the colonised Palestinian people? What would happen if these desires conflicted with those of the coloniser, as happened in 2006? All the messages sent to the White House did not help convince it to accept the results. Similarly, all the concessions made by the authority of 1996 did not contribute to convincing the Israeli occupier to live up to its commitments made in the signed accords, let alone under international law. The first PLC elections since 2006 were set for 2021 but then indefinitely postponed by the PA.

It is time to break idols and overcome illusions. This is the time of revolutions — the time of change in the Arab world. No election — if it is ever held — that takes place under occupation, colonisation, and apartheid, excluding most sectors of the Palestinian people, can be considered free. *If all Palestinians, especially in the Diaspora,* do not participate, the result is known in advance. The results can only serve the will and interests of the occupier, promoting further the fragmentation experienced by the Bantustan of the West Bank and Gaza, either through futile negotiations, lasting forever by design if the secular right wins, or through continued blockade and further genocidal wars, if the religious right again manages to surprise everybody. Either–or is the only choice we are given by the new PLC elections, which would, in any event, represent only a third of the Palestinian people.

The democratic alternative is one that reflects the collective will of the Palestinian people. This alternative lies in elections to the Palestinian National Council (PNC) after reconstructing the PLO on the basis of true democracy to ensure genuine representation of all national and Islamic factions. PNC elections will ensure the representation of the Diaspora away from the mentality of false independence cultivated under an oppressive occupier. These elections can bring the Palestinian people closer to self-determination, as defined by international law, while restoring their legitimate right to multiple forms of resistance.

We should not, therefore, repeat the same mistake for a third time by falling into the trap of PLC elections. The Palestinians of the Gaza Strip and the West Bank should *not* go to the polls again, even if the two rival factions reach such an agreement. Our registration at the polls should only work to advance simultaneous PNC elections after the removal of the Oslo leadership by dismantling the PA altogether. The Palestinian long walk to freedom cannot go hand in hand with false PLC elections under policies of occupation, colonisation, and Israeli apartheid. Only a new PNC, the Palestinian parliament, can be the sole legitimate representative of the entire Palestinian people.

What needs to be addressed at this moment in time is a historical human vision of the Palestinian question, a vision that never denies the rights of two-thirds of the Palestinian people, one that guarantees complete *equality* in historic Palestine, and abolishes apartheid —instead of recognizing a new Bantustan twenty years after the fall of apartheid in South Africa.

HAMAS'S ELECTORAL VICTORY

When Hamas unexpectedly won the 2006 elections in the West Bank and Gaza Strip, the message from the one-third of the Palestinian people living in those territories was clear: no more of the 'peace process' facade — with its untiring 'two-state solution' slogan that never materialised, and no more of the bread crumbs offered to the new inauthentic NGOized, Osloized leadership classes. (In the years since the 1993 Oslo Accords, funding NGOs has been a major means for foreign governments to influence, co-opt, and neutralise Palestinian politics. This process of 'Osloization' made some Palestinian organisations more loyal to their funders than to their principles.)

Many of those who voted Hamas into power were not, in fact, supporters of the organisation but rather disgruntled Palestinians looking for change and reform after thirteen years of futile, meaningless negotiations that did massive damage to the Palestinian cause and transformed it from a liberation struggle supported by millions all over the world into a dispute between 'two equal parties', two countries fighting for border arrangements.

Undoubtedly, Hamas's electoral victory turned the whole equation upside down and was considered a blow to the Bush doctrine in the Middle East. The price paid by the Palestinians of the West Bank and Gaza Strip has been hefty, not because of their support for Hamas but rather because of their choice to put an end to the 'peace process' charade. Had there been another Palestinian political force that could be trusted to fight the outcome of the Oslo Accords in a principled manner, it might have had a chance. But by 2006, the left had already gone through a process of NGOization and Osloization that put it to the right of Hamas, dovetailing with the right wing that was already in control of the PLO.

Hamas, then, won the elections because it was expected, whether rightly or wrongly, to rectify historic mistakes made by the official leadership — most importantly, defending the right of return of refugees and putting an end to the unattained two-state solution. A deadly, hermetic siege was imposed on the Palestinians of Gaza as soon as the election results came out, followed by numerous attempts to destabilise the situation through a US-backed coup attempt, culminating in Israel's 22-day genocidal war on Gaza.

The 2009 war was a political tsunami aimed at creating a sense of defeat amongst the Palestinians and a sense that they are confronted with a metaphysical power that can never be defeated, that their choice of an anti-Oslo political power was not only a political mistake but an existential one as well, a mistake that would change their future altogether, hence, the calculated targeting of children and families. More than 90 per cent of the victims of the massacre were civilians, according to leading human rights organisations. None of the declared objectives of the massacre, however, were achieved: Hamas remains in power, and the resilience of the Palestinians of Gaza is stronger than ever. Israel has failed to make them feel that they are a defeated people.

Hamas rallied tens of thousands of its supporters in celebrations of the 'historic victory over the Zionist entity'. Its spokespersons reiterated again and again that based on this historic victory, there would be no return to the pre-massacre siege and that reality on the ground now 'necessitated' new steps. The Palestinian people in the West Bank and Gaza Strip, the Diaspora and 1948 Palestine (the part of Palestine on which Israel was declared in 1948) also had high expectations. Gaza 2009 was rightly, expected to be the Sharpeville of Palestine, a turning point in the history of the Palestinian struggle against Israel's policy of occupation, colonisation, and apartheid.

This historic victory against Israel's aggression required visionary leadership, one with a clear-cut strategy of liberation that divorces itself completely from the Oslo Accords and the deceptive two-prison solution. Instead of building on this victory and the outpouring of international support in the streets of Istanbul, London, Amman, Caracas, Johannesburg, and even Muscat — to mention but a few cities — the leadership of the Palestinian resistance movement, including Hamas, rushed to Cairo in what turned out to be endless, futile rounds of national unity dialogue.

One is not, of course, against any serious attempt for national unity, but one also takes it for granted that the ABC of leadership, especially elected ones, is to be with the masses. The siege should have been exposed as the obstacle that prevents the leaders of the resistance from having national dialogue because they, as leaders, cannot and should not leave their besieged, traumatised people and move freely outside Gaza. This should have become a condition. If any Arab dignitary wanted to have a discussion with the victorious leadership, they should have been invited to Gaza. One would have expected the Gaza leadership to act as a victorious one, to wait in Gaza and make it clear that they would welcome any sign of genuine support and solidarity while they were staying with their people in Gaza.

This was a step in what I call the 'abortion of victory'. Instead of coming up with an alternative program to that of the PA and all the organisations belonging to it, and instead of building on the unprecedented, growing solidarity with the Palestinians of Gaza, the leadership of Hamas, in statements made by its leaders and — more importantly — letters sent to the US president, have started reinventing the wheel. I will limit myself to a couple of important examples: Hamas's flirtation with the administration and their endorsement of the two-prison solution.

Failing to understand that Obama's election did not represent a radical change in US Middle East policy was a sign of, to say the least, political immaturity. The 'diversity' within the US establishment is like the difference between the Likud and Labour parties in Israel. Obama and Joe Biden today still represent the Democratic Party, which is a part of the mainstream US establishment. Obama and Biden's victory in the presidential elections in 2008, therefore, did not produce a change in the nature of US imperialism. Obviously, Hamas bought the fiction brought about by the election of Obama and his 'seriousness' in resolving the Israeli-Palestinian conflict. Hamas failed to see that, in essence, what Obama was offering was not different from what George W. Bush and, before him, Bill Clinton offered. All US presidents have made it crystal clear that the US-Israel ties are 'unbreakable'. For the US administration, Israel's security remains the issue, which, ultimately, marginalises the whole issue of Palestine.

The Israeli-US siege imposed on Gaza would have been lifted immediately if Obama had decided it should be so. In fact, the US is not merely complicit but rather a participant in the war crimes and crimes against humanity committed against the Palestinians of Gaza. Any first-year student of political science, not to say a child on the streets of Gaza, would tell you this.

The second, more important example of Hamas's political immaturity is its acceptance of the already dead two-state solution. This is ironic, not to say bizarre, since every politician in Palestine knows that a two-state solution has been rendered impossible by Israeli colonisation of the West Bank, by the looting and pillaging of Gaza, by the construction of the apartheid wall, and by the expansion of so-called 'Greater Jerusalem'. Since 1967, the US has supported and is still supporting Israel in creating conditions that have made the two-state solution impossible, impractical, and unjust.

By launching its genocidal wars against Gaza, Israel has shot the two-state-prison solution in the head, which consequently means a dire need for an alternative program that addresses the Palestinian question as one of democracy, equality, human rights, and, ultimately, liberation from occupation, colonisation, and apartheid. Hamas, alas, has fallen within the trap of Oslo and its fetishisation of statehood at the expense of Palestinian fundamental rights. Of course, one tends to agree that the severe current crisis in Palestine emanates from the nature of the deformed political system created by the Oslo Accords and their claim of laying the foundation for a two-state solution. By participating in the January 2006 elections, most political organisations in Palestine, including Hamas, showed an implicit acceptance of the new political reality created by the Oslo Accords and, hence, the two-state solution. But, ironically, Hamas claimed otherwise, that its objective was to bring Oslo to an end.

But what does this state look like? And does Hamas have an alternative to the two-state, or two-prison, solution which has become impossible to achieve?

The experience of Hamas rule in the Gaza Strip offers a miniature model of an Islamic state, whereas the West Bank stands as the Bantustan state to be declared. It is common knowledge that Gaza has recently undergone ideological social transformations through laws that are enforced without being enacted. Such laws target individual freedoms, particularly those of women, who are no longer allowed to smoke water pipes in public or ride behind their spouses on motorcycles. Likewise, female students are now forced to wear the *jilbab* and the *hijab*, while female lawyers must wear the *hijab*. Of course, these practices claim to 'protect our customs and traditions', but is there a traditional text that bars women from smoking, for instance? The democracy that provided the foundation for the 2006 elections is based on guaranteeing individual freedoms. Many statements made by Hamas leaders inside and outside of Gaza before the elections emphasised that those leaders would respect such freedoms if elected.

The transformation of many members of the resistance, who are willing to sacrifice their lives for their homeland and who exerted impressive efforts to defend Gaza in 2009, into religious police like those in Saudi Arabia requires a serious and critical revision by Hamas.

Therefore, it is obvious that Hamas is unable to realise that the wars on Gaza have created a new political reality whereby Israel pulled the trigger on the racist two-state/two-prison solution. Hamas insists on adopting this approach and claims it is a temporary tactic until the balance of power shifts, as the movement assumes it will within the truce period of ten or twenty years. It plans to build a state after its model in Gaza during this time. This only indicates the lack of a clear strategic vision to end the conflict, a vision that draws on past global struggles against colonialism, particularly against the abhorrent South African apartheid regime, which collapsed resoundingly in 1994.

Unfortunately, there has been no indication, based on my reading of many statements made by Hamas leaders, of a clear understanding within the movement either of the apartheid nature of the State of Israel or of the tools used by the South African anti-apartheid movement. One such tool is the international boycott campaign, without which the apartheid regime would not have ended. This demonstrates Hamas's failure to understand the role of the BDS.

In a fashion similar to the boycott movement against the South African apartheid regime, the BDS movement is guided by a national boycott committee, the BDS National Committee (BNC), particularly the Palestinian Campaign for the Academic and Cultural Boycott of Israel (PACBI). The difference between the two experiences is that in South Africa, the United Democratic Front (UDF) — a broad coalition of civil society groups struggling against apartheid within South Africa — founded its movement on linking grassroots popular resistance with international solidarity. This was particularly true of the boycott campaign. The failure of both the nationalist and Islamist wings of the Palestinian leadership to study, build upon, and link this experience with the history of Palestinian resistance must also be rectified immediately.

However, it is evident that the development of an alternative leadership cannot wait. As a benchmark in the history of the

Palestinian struggle, the formation of the BNC, along with its main objectives, has reconnected the various segments of the Palestinian people to stand in the face of occupation, colonisation, and institutionalised racist discrimination against Palestinian citizens of Israel, and to call for the return of refugees. These indivisible demands distinguish the new alternative Palestinian strategy. Yet the question remains: is Gaza willing to constructively interact with such a positive development in the Palestinian struggle with openness to the other national players and without a narrow factional vision?

In the late 1980s, the Palestinian national movement accepted the two-state solution and, at a later stage, recognised Israel. This is the same resistance movement that in the 1960s emerged to liberate Palestine from the Jordan River to the Mediterranean Sea. Behind-the-scenes negotiations ultimately led to the signing of the notorious Oslo Accords, which paved the way for transforming the Palestinian cause into one of charity. Now, Hamas is reinventing the wheel. No wonder one has a sense of *déjà vu*.

DIS-PARTICIPATION AS A PALESTINIAN STRATEGY?

Many solutions have been put forward to the decades-long crisis of leadership afflicting the Palestinian people, such as reform of the PLO from within through elections to the PNC or by bringing Hamas and other Islamist groups into the PLO Executive Committee.

However, the crisis of the existing leadership and indeed of all political parties on the Right as well as on the Left is now so deeply ingrained that the only way forward may be to 'dis-participate' in the present Palestinian political system.

What is 'dis-participation'? As defined by Mas'ud Zavarsadeh and Donald Morton in a different context in their *Theory as Resistance*, 'the options come down to either being "persuaded" of the legitimacy of working within the system and thus accepting the existing structures, or finding that there is no space for radical change'. The problem of working within an existing system that has lost legitimacy is that it obscures what is '*possible* which is suppressed in the pragmatic *is*' as Zavarsadeh and Morton point out.

In order to spotlight the power of what is possible for the Palestinian people, we must first dis-participate in illegitimate political structures. Otherwise, we continue to face a very limited set of options, each worse than the other and none realising Palestinian self-determination and rights. This is not a call to end Palestinian activism for self-determination, freedom, justice, and equality — far from it, as will be discussed after a brief review of the crisis of the Right as well as the Left below.

THE CRISIS OF THE RIGHT

Applying the term 'illegitimate' to the entire Palestinian political system, including the political parties on both the Left and the Right, may sound too harsh or sweeping — until one examines the facts. I have recently written extensively about the crisis of the Right in both its secular and religious manifestations at Rai Alyoum and about the crisis of the Left at *al-Akhbar*.[4] The main points are worth noting. The crisis of the rightwing parties, both 'secular' (Fatah and its allies) and 'religious' (Hamas and its allies), is now more flagrant than ever. It is wrong to trace this crisis back to the 2007 confrontation between Fatah and Hamas, in large part engineered by the US, which led to the split between Gaza and the West Bank.

In fact, the crisis of the Right dates from the adoption of the PLO ten-point Interim Program of 1974 and the principle of establishing a national authority on any part of Palestine that was liberated. This, in turn, led to the concessions made in the Oslo Accords as of 1993. Thus, even if the Fatah-Hamas split were to

4 Haider Eid, 'The Palestinian Right and the New Dualities' (Arabic), *Rai Alyoum*, November 1, 2013.

be healed, as several government and civil society initiatives have attempted to do as a first step to righting the Palestinian body politic, this would not revive the Palestinian Right as an effective force for Palestinian self-determination and rights.

At this stage, both religious and secular Right are committed to the two-state project, which basically denies the Palestinian right of return and transforms the relationship between the Palestinians of the West Bank and Gaza, on the one hand, and the Palestinian refugees, exiles, and citizens of Israel on the other into one of 'solidarity'. As for the hoped-for state, should it come about, it would be no better than a Bantustan based on ethno-religious discrimination. Worse, the West Bank and Gaza have themselves now become two distinct parts.

The secular Palestinian Right and now the religious Right have basically fallen into the trap set decades ago by the Zionist left, which was willing to accept a Palestinian state along with a 'just solution' for the refugee question. This is the approach the PLO accepted in its Interim Program despite the contradictions between the establishment of an independent state on the 1967 borders and the right of return as well as the right to self-determination of the Palestinian people as a whole. Both the secular and the religious Right have made it a priority to establish relations with the US. The secular Right was successful, while the religious Right repeatedly sent messages about its willingness to accept a two-state solution and abide by a twenty-year truce, albeit without formally recognising Israel. Both sides have been willing to accept 'independence' in exchange for freedom. Neither has shown the capacity for creative, effective resistance. Their priority is to maintain their political existence in the form of two spineless authorities in two separate Bantustans. Their bankruptcy is compounded by the fact that Israel has made it crystal clear that its relentless colonisation project will continue.

THE OSLOIZED LEFT

The failures of the Right should not occasion too much surprise. It is the failures of the Left that cause pain and disappointment. The Left's deterioration followed its implicit acceptance of the Oslo Accords despite its alleged opposition. Both the Popular Front for the Liberation of Palestine (PFLP) and the Democratic Front for the Liberation of Palestine (DFLP) participated in the Legislative Council elections of 2006, thus providing legitimacy to one of the most important institutions of the Oslo Accords. They also tacitly accepted the two illegitimate PNC meetings held after Oslo was signed.

I should confess that I, like many residents of the West Bank and Gaza, naively thought that the Palestinian Left and other liberal forces would use this opening to strengthen and democratise the Palestinian national movement and weaken Fatah's authoritarian grip on the PLO. However, the Left's claim to represent the national aspirations of the people turned out to be hollow.

Most members of the political bureaus of the major Left parties are either directly employed by the PA/PLO or get paid monthly salaries without being directly employed. Can they make an honest or effective call for the dissolution of the PA, as some respected Palestinian activists and intellectuals urge? Meanwhile, many of those whom the PA does not employ have become directors of the mushrooming, Western-funded NGOs with all the strings and agendas that come with it. In short, instead of leading the efforts to fight the outcome of the Oslo Accords, most of the Left has, alas, been tamed by the Oslo Accords. It should be noted that not all the Left has gone this route, and a marginalised segment is seeking alternatives.

The Left's inexorable deterioration is perhaps best illustrated by the opportunistic and unprincipled position it adopted toward the standoff between Hamas and Fatah. Instead of respecting the outcome of the 2006 elections and supporting the formation of a united front with the party that won the elections with a clear majority on a platform of resistance and reforms, the Palestinian Left largely supported the unelected Ramallah government.

None of the PA's actions have motivated the Left to take a principled or effective position that would persuade the 'official leadership' of the PLO to reconsider its actions. The list is long and includes: the shutting down of charity organisations in the West Bank, the PA's imprisonment of political prisoners without trial or charge, the obstruction of the Goldstone Report at the United Nations Security Council (UNSC); and the brutal force with which the PA security forces attack anti-Oslo demonstrations, including those organized by left-wing organisations.

Even the PFLP, in theory, the most radical of the Left, turned a blind eye to the open secret of General Keith Dayton's widely circulated plan to orchestrate a *coup d'état* using the PA security forces against the Hamas government.[5] The PFLP, the DFLP, and the People's Party have not effectively protested the PLO's pro-US agenda and its repeated efforts at normalisation or those of its controlling party, Fatah.

Today, one must ask what still remains of the PLO and in fact, what remains of the Palestinian question at all. What rationale can the Palestinian Left possibly have for their ongoing commitment to a PLO that they say has been 'hijacked?'. However, I am aware that there is a big difference between the 'ancient' leaders of the left and the cadres who work on the ground, particularly the youth, although Fatah and Hamas still have a significant following, as university student council elections demonstrate. The question is, how can the youth be encouraged to effect change in such a bleak political environment? This question urgently requires an answer not just for the youth but for all those who still hold Palestinian national rights dear, and we are many. This is where the concept of 'dis-participation' can help.

5 David Rose, 'The Gaza Bombshell', *Vanity Fair*, April 2008.

DIS-PARTICIPATION: DECOLONIZING THE PALESTINIAN MIND

It is necessary to reject the existing system and its political and ideological bias and to reveal and oppose its exploitative, distortive, authoritarian features. This means putting the concept of 'dis-participation' into practice to reclaim Palestinian agency of the kind that will realise Palestinian national rights. To dis-participate is to put the legitimacy of the existing order at stake and, *at the same time*, to work for other alternatives and possibilities.

Many parties and individuals across the occupied territories are still calling for elections to the PLC n the occupied territories as the solution to all Palestinian problems. Really? The PLO has demanded that all factions accept the PA and participate in elections, forcing some organisations on the Left to falsely claim that elections for the PLC are a manifestation of plurality. The result is a situation in which political legitimacy is only granted to those who agree to work *within the system*. (Of course, the refugees and exiles were excluded from these elections.) This is not plurality.

There are already examples of how it is possible to dis-participate and yet to work toward realising Palestinian rights. The civil society-led movement for BDS until Israel recognises and upholds international law works outside the system and holds the system to account. The youth movement that took shape during the Arab uprisings is another way of dis-participating while working for rights. Another significant development in recent years is collective activism by Palestinians across all of historic Palestine, for example, in the determined_protests against Israel's attempts to ethnically cleanse the Negev Bedouin, the Unity Intifada, and the Sheikh Jarrah Hirak.

It is worth noting that representatives of the entire Palestinian political system — from Left to Right — are part of the BDS National Committee, where decisions are taken by consensus. In other words, even if political party leaders are now working in a deeply compromised system, the commitment to achieving Palestinian rights still runs deep amongst party cadres.

Of course, without a representative national movement in some shape or form, social movements cannot on their own achieve Palestinian rights, although they can help to ensure that these rights are not sold out.

The hope for such a national movement can only come from an alliance between the political party cadres still committed to Palestinian rights and the nascent Palestinian youth movement through a process of dis-participation that involves the rejection of the existing system and its replacement.

It is unlikely that change can come from the Right, but can we imagine a 'new' Left completely free from the Oslo legacy and providing a democratic alternative to the two-state industry? A Left that can really challenge the status quo and hold it accountable to Palestinian rights? Such a Left would have to *dis-participate* in the current establishment and:

1. Present its analysis of the current Palestinian situation and an alternative program. For example, if, as most of the ideologues of the Left have recently concluded, the two-state solution is dead, then what is their alternative? Continuing to pretend to accept a two-state solution as a step to the strategic goal of one state is like accepting the Bantustan system of apartheid South Africa as a step toward liberation.

2. Participate with other popular forces of resistance to strategise for international solidarity and boycott campaigns in a united front against the Zionist onslaught and upholding all Palestinian rights, including justice for Palestinian refugees, equality for the Palestinian citizens of Israel and their rights as an indigenous national minority, and freedom, including freedom from occupation, settler colonialism and siege.

3. Evolve an alternative economic vision to the neoliberal one practised and legitimated by the Palestinian right.

4. Tactically use the tools available to it. For example, elections have never taken place to elect the members of the PNC. This allows for the tactical move of resigning the party seats in the Executive Committee, which legitimates the concessions made by the controlling party but keeps the seats in an elected PNC. There are, of course, institutional limitations to the PNC's power — even an elected one — that will be exacerbated if the Left steps off the Executive Committee.

5. Study the experience of the Left in Latin America for comparative examples of how to re-energise the Palestinian Left.

Without these and other radical steps, there is no hope for the Palestinian Left, as Osamah Khalil put it in a different context:

Instead, much as they experienced in the PLO after 1988, the Palestinian Left's desperation for relevance will be used to further the agendas of stronger parties whose positions and platforms are antithetical to their own.

The above sets out a snapshot of some of the challenges faced by the Palestinian people and the call to address them through dis-participation in illegitimate structures. These preliminary ideas are intended to provoke debate and push forward thinking about alternatives to move beyond the existing system. There is no question that the creativity and determination the Palestinians have shown for close to a century will enable us to identify and realise those alternatives.

CHAPTER FIVE

Solidarity with Anti-Apartheid Resistance in Post-Oslo Palestine

The strategic value of international solidarity with the Palestinian people in the Gaza Strip and West Bank, refugees in the Diaspora, and Palestinians in Israel raises some fundamental questions. The most immediate and urgent are — what the nature of international solidarity should be and how it can best support the Palestinian struggle for self-determination.

International solidarity needs, first and foremost, to address the ways in which colonial Zionism has followed and continues to follow the Bantustanization policy of apartheid South Africa. There is also an imperative to address the severe damage that the Oslo Accords (1993) have caused to the Palestinian struggle, given the degree of confusion that these accords have created in the international arena.

HISTORICAL PARALLELS

A historical analysis of the current Palestinian quagmire cannot separate apartheid and Zionism from colonialism. As Samir Amin argues very persuasively in *Unequal Development*, in the nineteenth century South Africa, central capitalism and colonialists forcibly dispossessed rural African communities to satisfy their need for a large proletariat to exploit the country's great mineral wealth. The indigenous people were driven into barren regions, which left them with no alternative but to become cheap labour for European mines and farms and, later, rising South African industry. This initial dispossession slowly transformed a vibrant and dynamic society into mere labour reserves, with a gradual loss of independence and, ultimately, the creation of apartheid and Bantustans.

However, this process was not one-sided: throughout this dispossession and remaking of South Africa into a haven for racial supremacy, the international community was mobilised by the internal South African struggle to protest against apartheid's blatant creation of surplus labour, and against its inhuman and racist exploitation of Black South Africans.

Today, it is the Israeli apartheid state that is condemned for dispossessing and ethnically cleansing the native population. Israel has been accused of being worse than the apartheid state by South Africans such as Bishop Tutu, Blade Nzimande, and John Dugard. These South Africans who experienced apartheid cite Israel's use of F-16s and helicopter gunships on unarmed civilians, as well as the home demolitions and arrests of families of suspected 'militants' as practices that make Israeli apartheid qualitatively worse than that of South Africa.[1]

Similarities between the two apartheid states can be found in their policies on citizenship, their use of detention without trial, and laws which limit freedom of movement and the right to live in one's own home with one's family. Just as apartheid South Africa gave citizenship to white South Africans and relegated Blacks to 'independent homelands' (i.e. Bantustans), Zionism gives all Jews the right to citizenship in the State of Israel while denying citizenship to Palestinians — the indigenous inhabitants of the

1 Yitzhak Loav, 'Israel's Apartheid is Worse Than South Africa's', *Haaretz*, November 6, 2009.

land. While apartheid used race to determine citizenship, the state of Israel used religious identification. Just as the apartheid state made laws criminalising the free movement of Blacks on their ancestral land, Israel uses a military occupation infrastructure composed of checkpoints, Jewish-only settlements and roads, the apartheid wall, plus a myriad of legal regulations that govern Palestinian daily life and are explicitly designed to restrict how they work and live.

Since 1967, Israel has detained a quarter of the Palestinian male population and today has over 5,200 prisoners in its jails, thousands of whom have no legal recourse.[2] Many of those incarcerated have spent years in jail for 'crimes' such as entering Israel illegally. Thousands of Palestinian families live with the threat of forced separation or are already separated because they do not have the necessary permits to live together — permits Israel has refused to issue since 2000. These policies strike at the heart of family life since Palestinians are forced to apply to Israel for family reunification permits if they want to live together.

During the years of apartheid, South Africa came under repeated pressure from the international community and multilateral organisations such as the UNSC, which passed countless resolutions against it because of its inhumane treatment of Blacks. This gave much-needed succour to the oppressed, while Palestinians today are bereft of even this tiny comfort because the US continues to use its veto to ensure that Israel escapes censure from the world body.

Over the decades, international solidarity with the Palestinian people has played an extremely important, albeit dialectical, role in enhancing the struggle. There is an undeniable correlation between the different forms of struggle in the occupied territories

2 ADDAMEER (Arabic for conscience) Prisoner Support and Human Rights Association is a Palestinian non-governmental, civil institution that works to support Palestinian political prisoners held in Israeli and Palestinian prisons. The data is updated on their website.

and the international attention and solidarity it is able to command. Disturbingly, after 20 years of Israel side-stepping every commitment made in the Oslo Accords, there still strongly lingers in international civil society a belief that the Palestinian struggle has, in essence, been resolved. Hence the urgency for an international solidarity campaign that will highlight the similarities between apartheid and Zionism, as well as the common experience of Palestinians today as dispossessed people and Black South Africans under apartheid.

South Africans had to wait twenty-seven years for their chosen leader and political party to be free to lead them; during those long years, they rejected all false leaders that were foisted on them even when the likes of Margaret Thatcher and Ronald Reagan celebrated these quislings. As late as 1987, Thatcher was confident enough to say that 'Nelson Mandela would never be the president of a free South Africa'.

Like Thatcher's government, other governments around the world were forced to end their support for apartheid South Africa. They would not have done so without the pressure exerted on them by their own people. Israel needs to be isolated in exactly the same way as apartheid South Africa. Today, there is a growing mass-based struggle inside Palestine, as well as other forms of struggle, exactly as there was inside apartheid South Africa. An intensified international solidarity movement with a common agenda can make the struggle for Palestine resonate in every country in the world, thus closing off the world to Israelis until they open the world to Palestinians.

THE GAZA BANTUSTAN

The Palestinian national movement has overlooked this question: does the Gaza Strip resemble the racist Bantustans of apartheid South Africa? During the apartheid era, South Africa's Black population was kept in isolation and without political and civil rights. Is Gaza similar? The answer is Yes and No.

What is apartheid? As defined by the 1973 United Nations Convention (UN General Assembly Resolution 3068), apartheid is a policy of racial or ethnic segregation founded on a set of discriminatory practices that favour a specific group in order to ensure its racial supremacy over another group. In Israel, institutionalised racial discrimination is unequivocally founded on ensuring the primacy of a group of Jewish settlers over the Palestinian Arabs. When comparing the applications of the apartheid policy, it is difficult to identify any differences between white rule in South Africa and its Israeli counterpart in Palestine in terms of the segregation and designation of certain areas to Israeli Jews and others to the Arabs, the delineation of certain laws and privileges for Jews, and a discriminatory set of laws that apply only to Palestinians.

Currently, in both Israel and the occupied Palestinian territories, there are two road systems, two housing systems, two educational systems, and different legal and administrative systems for Jews and non-Jews. Every law enacted during the South African apartheid system has a corresponding law in Israel. This includes the Group Areas Act, the Prohibition of Mixed Marriages Act, the Law on Movement and Permits, the Public Safety Act, the Population Registration Act, the Immorality Act, the Land Act and, of course, the Bantu Homelands Citizenship Act. The corresponding Israeli laws are the Law of Return, the 2003 'temporary' laws prohibiting mixed marriages, the Population Registry Law, the Citizenship and Entry into Israel Law, the Israeli Nationality Law, and land and property laws.

Like South Africa, Israel's brand of apartheid is mixed with settler colonialism. As in the US and Australia, settler colonialism in Israel and South Africa has also involved the ethnic cleansing or 'incremental genocide' of the indigenous people influenced by a racist and/or religious ideology of supremacy.

When evaluated along these lines, the term apartheid clearly applies to Israeli policies in the Gaza Strip. The Palestinians of the Gaza Strip are isolated from the rest of the population in historical Palestine and do not enjoy minimum political rights and basic living conditions available to Jewish residents because they were born to mothers from the 'wrong' religion. In this context, it should be recalled that 80 per cent of the population in the Strip were ethnically cleansed in 1948 and are barred from returning to the villages and cities from which they were driven out.[3]

The Bantustans were part of apartheid South Africa's racist formula to separate the Black population and preserve white supremacy. Although the Bantustans were called 'independent homelands', their inhabitants were not granted equal rights or even independent political decision-making power — a harbinger of what was planned for the so-called independent Palestinian state within the June 1967 borders. In South Africa, the debate was about eleven states that could live side by side in peace. Despite Pretoria's best efforts, the Bantustans gained no international recognition.

Gaza, however, is deprived of even this racist formula. As Saree Makdisi maintains, Israel appears to have learned a lesson from South Africa.[4] It did not appoint local leaders to provide 'limited self-government' over the West Bank and Gaza. Rather, in coordination with the US and shielded by the international community, Israel allowed 'free' elections to take place so that the Bantustanisation process could gain 'legitimacy' and international approval as an allegedly independent Palestinian state. Although hailed internationally, the elections which took place under occupation were a Palestinian tragedy. Israel succeeded in enticing the indigenous people in Palestine to promote the illusion of potential 'independence' for segments of 22 per cent of historical Palestine.

---

3 Jean-Pierre Filiu, *Gaza : A History*, Oxford: Oxford University Press, 2014.
4 Saree Makdisi, 'The Architecture of Failure', *Critical Inquiry*, vol. 36, issue 3, Spring 2010.

GAZA UNDER SIEGE

At the same time, the answer to the question of whether 'apartheid' applies to Gaza is also *no*. The Gaza Strip has devolved from being a Bantustan during the Oslo Accord years (1993-2002) into a large concentration camp. Makdisi argues that the difference between the two kindred regimes — Israel and apartheid South Africa — is 'the difference between inferiority and dehumanisation'. He goes further and explains it as the 'difference between exploitation and genocide'.

Never, throughout the history of apartheid in South Africa, did the armed forces use the full force of their military against the civilian population in townships. In contrast, since the outbreak of the second Palestinian *Intifada* in September 2000 and culminating in the 2009, 2012, 2014, 2021, and 2023 invasions, Gaza has been attacked by F-16s, Apache helicopter gunships, warships, Merkava Tanks, and internationally prohibited phosphorus bombs.

Israel's siege on Gaza was imposed after Palestinians elected Hamas in internationally sanctioned and observed elections in 2006. It was tightened after Hamas defeated forces loyal to Fatah in June 2007. Since then, the list of items banned from entering Gaza covered more than 200 articles, including cement, paper, cancer medications, and even, pasta and chocolate. According to the Israeli organisation Gisha-Legal Center for Freedom of Movement, Israel granted access to only 97 articles, compared to 4,000 before the blockade. About 80 per cent of the Gaza Strip's population survives on humanitarian aid. More than 90 per cent of Gaza's factories have been shut down.[5]

When the 18-month-old siege failed to break the will of Palestinians in Gaza, Israel launched its deadly invasion at the end of 2008. According to human rights organisations and the UN-sanctioned Goldstone report (2009), more than 1,400 Palestinians,

5 See https://gisha.org/en/ for statistics and news.

including more than 300 children, were killed and thousands wounded. Israel destroyed at least 11,000 homes, 105 factories, 20 hospitals, and clinics, as well as 159 schools, universities, and technical institutes. Furthermore, it resulted in the displacement of 51,800 persons, of whom thousands remain homeless due to the following Israeli onslaughts in 2012, 2014, and 2021.

Commenting on this situation, Karen AbuZayd, former Commissioner-General for UNRWA, the UN agency for Palestine refugees, said: 'Gaza is on the threshold of becoming the first territory to be intentionally reduced to a state of abject destitution with the knowledge, acquiescence and — some would say — encouragement of the international community'.[6]

LEARNING FROM THE SOUTH AFRICAN ANTI-APARTHEID MOVEMENT

There is an urgent need, at this historic moment, to reshape international public opinion that is supportive of the Palestinian cause with emphasis on the multiple similarities between Zionism and the apartheid regime in South Africa. This can be accomplished by focusing on the common suffering of the indigenous Black population and the Palestinians today, not only in the West Bank and the Gaza Strip but also in the Palestinian Diaspora and inside Israel.

It is unfortunate that the 'official' Palestinian leadership has not studied and learned lessons from the South African experience. On the contrary, they almost unanimously accepted the creation of a type of Bantustan-based system that the anti-apartheid movement in South Africa rejected. One wonders the real reason behind this deliberate disregard of a very rich experience. Does it derive from the same misguided notion as that of the Bantustan leaders who claimed African racial nationalism? Does it involve chauvinism

6 Karen Koning AbuZayd, 'The Brutal Siege of Gaza Can Only Breed Violence', *The Guardian*, January 23, 2008.

and a lack of openness to other people's experiences? Is our cause really so exceptional from a historical point of view that we must accept racist structures promoted as an 'autonomous' solution?

Unfortunately, the struggle for liberation has been reduced to one for Bantustans. In other words, the consciousness of the Palestinian struggle has split as a result of fetishising the concept of state at the expense of liberation, nullifying the right of return without saying so, and the tiresome reiteration of the 'Palestinian national project'. This stands in conflict with the aspirations of the vast majority of the Palestinian people, who are refugees, guaranteed the right of return under international law.

The option of an independent Palestinian state has become impossible for several reasons, including Israel's endeavours to transform settlements into cities, increase the number of settlers to more than half a million, build the apartheid wall in the occupied West Bank, expand Greater Jerusalem and cleanse it of its Palestinian inhabitants, and systematically turn Gaza into the largest detention centre on the face of the Earth. It is obvious that the Palestinian national movement as a whole has been infected with the virus of the Oslo Accords. The Oslo virus creates false consciousness that transforms the struggle for liberation, the return of refugees, human rights, and full equality into a struggle for 'independence' with limited sovereignty: a flag, a national anthem, and a small piece of land on which to exercise municipal sovereignty and establish ministries, all with the permission of the occupier.

The other side of the Palestinian leadership, i.e. Hamas, frequently proposes 10-year and 20-year truces, arguing that the truce is an 'alternative' to the demise of the two-state solution. Although there are no significant differences between these two sides in terms of the principle of accepting a purely nationalist solution to the Palestinian cause, this minor disagreement has gained greater prominence and has been employed to serve the racist two-state dogma. The so-called 'alternative' of a 20-year truce bets that the pragmatic nature of this call will 'persuade' the international community. In fact, it lacks a clear strategic vision to resolve the conflict in a way that ensures the return of refugees. What does a 20-year truce mean? Isn't this a message to the refugees to endure another 20 years until the balance of power shifts? What happens if it does not shift?

The two-state solution has unfortunately become the prevailing political discourse over the past two decades. Some traditionally leftist intellectuals, having been transformed into a socially and politically right-wing or 'neo-liberal' left, defend this solution as the only one available given the prevailing balance of power. They also defend it as a transitional or interim scheme. They occasionally threaten to espouse the one-state settlement, using this as a scarecrow not only to frighten Israel but also against us, the indigenous population. These attempts reveal an ideological decline and a lack of faith in the ability of the Palestinian people and the broader international solidarity movements to make revolutionary changes like those that took place against the apartheid regime. My contention is that the tools of resistance adopted by the anti-apartheid movement give the Palestinians valuable lessons to learn from. This, however, does not by any means signify a cut-and-paste approach. Those who are unfamiliar with the South African political map should not get the impression that the South African approach is *the* 'correct' solution to the Palestinian problem. Turning power over from white to black hands has, in fact, helped many apartheid perpetrators to get away with their crimes literally.

To avoid the pitfalls of national consciousness, Frantz Fanon rightly argues immediate steps should be taken toward political and social consciousness after independence. Has this happened in South Africa? In John Pilger's words, 'revolution [in South Africa] has been betrayed!' The betrayal of the Black masses, corruption, privatisation, lack of government intervention in fighting AIDS, poverty and crime, and deterioration of education in Black townships — are just a few symptoms of a still divided and economically troubled country.

In fact, the inconsistency of the ANC corresponds to that of the petty bourgeoisie. This is why it has shown itself in the end to be conservative with regard to the main problems, like other traditionally 'white' parties, and why it does not give any thought to land reforms, for example, not to mention nationalisation.

Any critical perspective shows how the interests of the previous controlling class are protected and reconciled with the revolutionary past of the new Black middle class. One wonders whether there are any fundamental differences between the reformist program that led to the emergence of a 'new' South Africa and the ideological program that many white South African investment bankers and capitalists undertook. Substantially, the same program has been supported by the ANC-led government. What it has rejected is not apartheid as such, but rather its legal apparatus that was imposed to facilitate the extraction of surplus labour.

The program of the ANC-led government tends to obscure class relations by moralising race over class. Thus, the current regime does not represent a radical change in class relations, but rather a modification of the social relations of capital. The racist extraction of surplus value has, in other words, become 'human', 'liberal', and most importantly, 'Black'. This is what the Palestinian anti-apartheid movement should take into consideration.

In a short story entitled 'The Music of the Violin', by South African writer Njabulo Ndebele, one of the characters comments on the 'concessions' made by the apartheid regime to indigenous people: 'That's how it is planned. That we be given a little of everything, and so prize the little we have that we forget about freedom'. In that same story, a Black revolutionary intellectual says that he'd 'rather be a hungry dog that runs freely in the streets, than a fat, chained dog burdened with itself and the weight of the chain'. These two voices from South Africa summarise the lessons colonised Palestinians should learn. There was no potential for coexistence with apartheid in South Africa, and Palestinians should accept no less, heeding the advice of the late visionary Palestinian intellectual Edward Said:

Equality or Nothing!

CONCLUSION

An Alternative Vision

Many articles have already been written criticising the normalisation deal signed between the United Arab Emirates (UAE), Bahrain, and Israel and calling it a stab in the back of the Palestinian people. Others have argued that it should not have come as a surprise since the ruling oligarchies in the UAE and Bahrain have been in bed with apartheid Israel for years, and it was only a matter of time before they made it public in order to strengthen their alliance against the two main threats: Iran and the spread of democracy in the Arab world.

This book does not go down the same path. Rather, it is an attempt to engage with what seems to be a social, political, economic, and historical formulation of an alternative programme to what is offered by the hegemonic imperialist, zionist, and reactionary powers.

In this context, it is useful to bring up US literary critic Fredric Jameson's theorisation of 'cognitive mapping', a process that repeats, adds, and respects very strongly the laws of dialectics (the development and movement of opposites). In other words, interpreting normalisation deals by only understanding the historical context within which they were signed is not enough; one needs to offer a progressive programme that challenges them on the basis of changing the conditions which have ultimately led to them, namely settler-colonialism and apartheid in Palestine.

The signing of the deal between Israel, Bahrain, and the UAE at the White House on September 15 is, admittedly, the beginning of a new era that has started in the Middle East; however, it will not bring about — with its unbalanced power relations — a just solution to the Palestinian question.

The accords of Camp David (1979), Oslo (1993), Wadi Araba (1994), and the Abraham Accord (2020), all of which were borne out of trade deals and backroom diplomacy between Israel and those Arab countries, have sold out the Palestinian cause altogether. None of them addressed the basic Palestinian rights, like the right of return of the refugees, self-determination, equality, and freedom.

In a nutshell, all mentioned agreements have guaranteed Israeli control over historic Palestine from the Jordan River to the Mediterranean Sea, a *de facto* reality created by the stronger colonial party with no compromise whatsoever.

The current situation is undoubtedly the product of international and regional imbalances prevailing at this specific moment, which is neither static nor eternal but rather passing and will inevitably be followed by other moments, according to the law of dialectics.

There is no doubt, then, that this specific historical moment is the climax of Palestinian and Arab passivity because of the weakening of progressive Arab nationalism and the fall of the Palestinian right-wing leadership into the trap of the 'peace industry'. However, any approaching moment is expected to be heading against what is being offered to us under these circumstances: 'All that is solid melts into air' as Karl Marx wrote.

Opposition to the deals in the Arab world, in general, and the Gulf states, in particular, will grow exactly the same way the Egyptian and Jordanian peoples opposed and fought against the Camp David and Taba talks.

The alternative vision Palestinians have to embrace is a

geopolitical production that challenges the space newly drawn by the US, Israel, and their Arab allies — the so-called new Middle East — and puts forward a new map of secular-democratic Palestine in the heart of a democratic Arab world.

We need an alternative representation of the whole sociopolitical 'reality' currently rising in the area, which moves away from the much-repeated mantra of the racist two-state solution.

Palestinians need to move on but with new ideas emanating from a strong belief that '[wo]men make history, but they do not make it in circumstances chosen by themselves', as Marx has put it. For far too long, Palestinians have been led by right-wing politicians who have failed to achieve a single basic right of any of the three components comprising the Palestinian people: those living in the Diaspora, residents of Gaza and the West Bank, and second-class Palestinian citizens of Israel.

Hence, there is a need to stress the importance of Palestinian agency with a progressive leadership that is against all forms of class exploitation, whether national, sexual, or religious, a leadership that is necessarily secular in its deep understanding of the Palestinian question.

Such leadership cannot entertain racist solutions. It has to rise to the historical challenges posed by the new-old alliance of Israel, the US and reactionary Arab regimes and, thus, become an agent for activities of local, national, and international character through the promotion of BDS against Israel until it complies with international law.

There is an urgent need for a move beyond the present historical stage that is characterised by a form of prevailing nationalist dogmatism represented in slogans such as 'two states for two peoples' and 'the only solution is the two-state solution', and others. Such slogans, in a way, are the product of waves of normalisation with apartheid Israel, a process of remoulding the Arab and Palestinian mind through 'ideological state apparatuses', such as media, education, mosques, law, which try to manipulate and reshape the consciousness of individuals, especially of those with revolutionary potential.

There is also an urgent need for a departure from the nihilistic mood that has been dominating much of the Palestinian left-wing discourse lately by emphasising the importance of human agency and the necessity for a historical understanding of the current post-Oslo historical moment.

We need an alternative vision that can lead to peace and justice. And it seems that colonised Palestinians are meant to be the ones to offer a vision that rehumanizes them and their oppressors. That is their moral responsibility, being at the receiving end of a multitiered system of settler-colonial oppression.

When things looked so bleak for Black Africans suffering at the hands of another settler-colonial power, in a similar situation to what the Palestinians are going through, Nelson Mandela offered this alternative vision:

> I have fought against white domination, and I have fought against Black domination. I have cherished the ideal of a democratic and free society in which all persons live together in harmony and with equal opportunities. It is an ideal which I hope to live for and to achieve.

The alternative for Palestinians has to be one secular democratic state in historic Palestine, a state in which all citizens are treated equally regardless of their religion, gender, and colour. This state has to embrace the return of refugees and self-determination, both of which are a step towards solving the Palestinian and the Jewish questions. This is what the Palestinian people have to strive for — to turn the whole hegemonic political equation upside down.

VICTORIA BRITTAIN

Afterword

It took a Palestinian professor of English and Comparative Literature during his lifetime of exile in the West to disrupt the Western conversation about Palestine thirty years ago in the wake of the much-praised 1993 Oslo agreement between Israel and the Palestinian leadership. Edward Said famously forecast failure:

> Franz Fanon was right when he said to Algerians in 1960 that just to substitute an Algerian policeman for a French one is not the goal of liberation: a change in consciousness is.[1]

Now, another professor of literature in exile from his family home in the ethnically cleansed village of Zarnouqa, and immured in Gaza for close to two decades, has built on Edward Said's writings a new legacy with this book. Haider Eid is proposing nothing less than the 'change in consciousness' of Said's quotation from Fanon. This voice from Gaza speaks to Palestinians and to a West which knows nothing of Gaza beyond occasional TV images of horror. Eid's slim book calls for a wholly new strategy for guaranteeing basic Palestinian rights and a futuristic pursuit of a just peace.

---

1 Edward W. Said, *The End of the Peace Process: Oslo and After*, London: Pantheon Books, 2000.

These are themes laid out in much Palestinian academic work, for instance, in the website analyses and discussions in *al-Shabaka*.[2]

Senior Palestinians, including the national poet Mahmoud Darwish; the PLO foreign minister Farouk al-Kaddoumi; Professor (Emeritus) Nasser Aruri (who wrote two critical books on the subject of the Oslo agreement); Gaza's Dr Haider Abdel-Shafi, who led the Palestinian delegation to the Madrid talks which paved the way to Oslo; and Edward Said, were a significant current of post-Oslo pessimism.[3]

With an overwhelming Western governmental, media, and popular celebratory response to 'peace', also seen initially in Ramallah and other places in Palestine, their critique did not dent a hyper-positive narrative on Oslo's outcome of a two-state solution with 'Gaza and Jericho first'. Said had a well-known voice in the West — and his critiques of how Palestinian realities worsened thereafter, and in particular of the US role — made him the target of extremely harsh criticism in power circles, their media echoes, academia, and much of interested civil society.

Symbolic of the new times was that Palestine was to have its very own airport. Yasser Arafat International Airport was built near Rafah in the southern Gaza Strip and was completed in record time by Palestinian building companies — a symbol of Palestinian pride. It operated with acclaim for two years. But in December 2001, Israel bombed the airport's radar station and control tower, and the following month, Israeli army bulldozers destroyed the runway.

Bombing and bulldozing of homes, hospitals, schools, infrastructure, and olive and fruit trees have become part of

---

2 Leila Farsakh, *al-Shabaka*, 'Palestine Beyond Partition and the Nation-State', May 4, 2022. For more, please refer to: Leila Farsakh, *Rethinking Statehood in Palestine: Self-Determination and Decolonisation beyond Partition*, University of California Press, 2022.

3 Avi Shlaim, 'The Rise and Fall of the Oslo Peace Process' in *International Relations of the Middle East*, edited by Louise Fawcett, Oxford University Press, 2005.

Gaza's children's lives ever since. The Palestinian leadership has been arrested or assassinated. But, thirty years later, the pretense of a two-state solution lives on in the speeches of every Western politician.

Dr Eid, Associate Professor of Post-Colonial and Postmodern Literature, is a voice of witness and authority from Al-Aqsa University inside the unprecedented siege of Gaza. He was born in a refugee camp in Gaza, far from the family home in the village of Zarnouqa (in what became Israel), which he visited only once as a child, and brought up in Gaza City. He did his first and second degrees in Cyprus at the Eastern Mediterranean University and spent three years at the University of Johannesburg doing a PhD. It was the late 1990s, and South Africa was still in the glow of excitement at the country's transformation from the overthrow of apartheid. Those years gave him a vision of monumental success achieved with a high price paid in blood and sacrifice. Against all the odds in a Cold War world where the weight of the West was firmly behind the apartheid regime, South Africa's struggle for Black majority rights struck a chord that echoes with his life experience.

Dr Eid returned to Palestine in 2000, hoping to work in the West Bank universities of Birzeit or An-Najah, but the Israelis refused him a permit, and he spent a year in Gaza working at Al-Quds Open University. Then, he went back to South Africa for a couple of years. He could have stayed, but Gaza drew him back as the aftermath of the Second Intifada became Gaza's reality.

In his 1993 Reith Lectures, Said's characterisation of the intellectual as 'exile and marginal, as amateur, and as the author of a language that tries to speak the truth to power' applies as well to Eid as to himself.[4] 'The intellectual always has a choice either to side with the weaker, the less-represented, the forgotten or ignored, or to side with the more powerful', Said goes on. Gaza, in

4 Edward W. Said, *Representations of the Intellectual:1993 Reith Lectures*, Vintage, Random House, 1994.

the violent days of death, maiming, and imprisonment from the Second Intifada, was Eid's choice of side.

To situate Haider Eid today, his automatically generated email response is a good place to start:

> I am currently living in Gaza, which has been under a barbaric, Israeli siege for more than 15 years. The worst aspect of this hermetic blockade is a constant power outage! Please be understanding if I do not respond immediately. I am doing my best!

Two years ago, Gaza was set to become unliveable, according to a sober UN study from 2012 citing the grim effects of the Israeli siege since 2007 on the stressed economy, acute unemployment, extreme shortage of clean water, constricted electricity supply, and health care structures strained beyond measure. The year 2020 came and went as those desperate realities continued their inexorable de-development of Gaza, intensified by five major Israeli military offensives beginning in 2008-09 known as Operation Cast Lead.[5]

The texture of life lies today, as yesterday, in acute poverty and the memories of days and nights of terror — assassinations of political leaders and others like the four young boys from the Bakr family targeted as they played on the beach, the entire families killed while they ate or slept together as Israeli bombs shattered whole neighbourhoods from Beit Lahiya in the north, through Shuja'iyya and the centre of Gaza City to Rafah in the south.

But still, Gaza lives and produces a book like this. Culture and imagination flourish, making it likely that Haider Eid's voices will find receptive ears. (He is also a musician.) Young Gazans have seized the opportunities of social media to open virtual doors to the world, including the West. Thanks to Gaza's prolific artists,

---

5 Jean-Pierre Filiu in *Journal of Palestine Studies* Vol 45, No 3 – Spring 2016 reviewed the 3rd edition of Sara Roy's *Gaza Strip - the Political Economy of De-Development* first published in 1995.

photographers, and filmmakers, everyone can see children's choirs, orchestras and soloists singing and playing on the beach or in studios; *dabka* dance groups; singers; actors; clowns in classrooms and kindergartens; artwork including huge murals painted on the walls of Khan Yunis refugee camp and in Gaza City; short stories, videos and poems by young Gazans published by the group *We Are Not Numbers*.[6]

Two young Gazan writers, Heba Hayak and Mosab Abu Tolba, won the Creative Award at the Palestine Book Awards in London in late 2022; a group of university students ran a French language radio programme; Nidaa Badwan's photographic series *One Hundred Days of Solitude* was shown in the French Institute in Jerusalem; and health professionals from Gaza such as psychiatrist Dr Yasser Abu-Jamei, director of the Gaza Community Mental Health Programme, writes, speaks, and links with colleagues in the profession in the US and UK in open zoom meetings.

Edward Said has been dead for twenty years. Every year, Said memorial lectures are held in many cities and universities. In the 2022 lecture in London, the Nobel Literature Prize winner Abdulrazak Gurnah noted the key role his students at the British University in Kent gave to Said. Haider Eid calls Said 'the spiritual figurehead of the Palestinian Cultural landscape'. Palestinians treasure Said for his relentless truth-telling of Palestinian realities that have brought some change in consciousness. This urgent book from Gaza calls for such a consciousness change in a new period of unprecedented pressure on Palestinian culture, identity, and futures.

---

6 We Are Not Numbers (WANN) is a youth-led Palestinian nonprofit project in the Gaza Strip. It tells the stories behind the numbers of Palestinians in the news and advocates for their human rights. WANN was founded and conceived in early 2015 by the American journalist Pam Bailey.

HAIDAR EID

is Associate Professor of Postcolonial
and Postmodern Literature at Gaza's al-Aqsa University.
He is the author of *'Worlding' Postmodernism:
Interpretive Possibilities of Critical Theory*
and *Countering the Palestinian Nakba:
One State for All.*

VICTORIA BRITAIN

has worked as a journalist in
Saigon, Algiers, Angola and Palestine, among many
places in the Global South, for UK, French and US
media. She has written books and plays about
Southern Africa, Guantanamo, and the impact of the war
on terror on women. Her most recent book is
Love and Resistance in the Films of Mai Masri.